STERLING BIOGRAPHIES

MUHAMMAD ALI

King of the Ring

D0451800

Stephen Timblin

STERLING

New York / London
www.sterlingpublishing.com/kids

Thanks, as always, to Sandra, Annalia, and Matilde

STERLING and the distinctive Sterling logo are registered trademarks of
Sterling Publishing Co., Inc.

Library of Congress Cataloging-in-Publication Data
Timblin, Stephen.
  Muhammad Ali : king of the ring / by Stephen Timblin.
    p. cm. — (Sterling biographies)
  Includes bibliographical references and index.
  ISBN 978-1-4027-7152-1 (hardcover) — ISBN 978-1-4027-6364-9 (pbk.)
  1. Ali, Muhammad, 1942—Juvenile literature. 2. Boxers (Sports)—United States—
Biography—Juvenile literature. I. Title.
  GV1132.A4T56 2010
  796.83092—dc22
  [3]
                                                        2009024238

Lot #: 10 9 8 7 6 5 4 3 2 1
12/09

Published by Sterling Publishing Co., Inc.
387 Park Avenue South, New York, NY 10016
© 2010 by Stephen Timblin

Distributed in Canada by Sterling Publishing
c/o Canadian Manda Group, 165 Dufferin Street
Toronto, Ontario, Canada M6K 3H6
Distributed in the United Kingdom by GMC Distribution Services
Castle Place, 166 High Street, Lewes, East Sussex, England BN7 1XU
Distributed in Australia by Capricorn Link (Australia) Pty. Ltd.
P.O. Box 704, Windsor, NSW 2756, Australia

Printed in China

Sterling ISBN 978-1-4027-7152-1 (hardcover)
         ISBN 978-1-4027-6364-9 (paperback)

Image research by Jim Gigliotti and James Buckley, Jr.

For information about custom editions, special sales, premium and corporate
purchases, please contact Sterling Special Sales Department at 800-805-5489
or specialsales@sterlingpublishing.com.

Contents

Events in the Life of Muhammad Ali (Cassius Clay)

1942

January 17, 1942
Cassius Marcellus Clay, Jr., is born to Cassius Marcellus Clay, Sr., and Odessa Grady Clay in Louisville, Kentucky. He is the first of two sons.

August/September 1960
At eighteen years old, Clay wins a gold medal as a Light heavyweight boxer at the Rome Olympics.

November 15, 1962
With a record of 15–0, Clay fights his one-time trainer Archie Moore. Clay predicts before the fight that he'll win in the fourth round, and he does just that.

March 6, 1964
In a radio broadcast, Elijah Muhammad, leader of the Nation of Islam, announces that Cassius Clay has changed his name to Muhammad Ali.

June 19, 1967
At a trial for refusing induction into the U.S. Army, Ali is found guilty and receives the maximum sentence—five years in jail and a $10,000 fine. His lawyers appeal the case, keeping him out of jail.

October 26, 1970
Ali returns to the ring for his first fight in three and a half years. He defeats Jerry Quarry in front of a star-studded crowd in Atlanta, Georgia.

June 28, 1971
The U.S. Supreme Court unanimously reverses Ali's previous conviction for refusing induction into the U.S. Army.

January 28, 1974
Ali and Frazier battle for the second time. Ali avenges his first loss by defeating Frazier.

October 1, 1975
Ali battles Joe Frazier for a third and final time in the Thrilla in Manila in the Philippines.

September 1984
Ali is officially diagnosed with Parkinson's syndrome.

July 19, 1996
Ali lights the Olympic Torch—and receives a tremendous ovation—to open the Olympic Games in Atlanta, Georgia.

October 1954
After his bike is stolen, twelve-year-old Clay meets a police officer who encourages him to start training as a boxer. Six weeks later, he wins his first bout.

October 29, 1960
Clay makes his professional boxing debut in his hometown of Louisville, squaring off against Tunney Hunsaker. Clay beats Hansaker in a six-round decision.

February 25, 1964
Cassius Clay defeats Sonny Liston in Miami to become the Heavyweight champion of the world.

April 28, 1967
Ali officially refuses to join the U.S. Army at the U.S. Armed Forces Examining and Entrance Station in Houston, Texas. One hour later, the New York State Athletic Commission suspends his boxing license.

June 1968
Ali and his second wife, Belinda Boyd, have a daughter named Maryum. She is the first of his eventual nine children.

March 8, 1971
Ali and Joe Frazier battle for the first of three times. Frazier wins the fifteen-round fight by unanimous decision, handing Ali his first professional loss.

March 31, 1973
Ali loses to the relatively unknown Ken Norton.

October 30, 1974
Ali wins back the Heavyweight championship by defeating George Foreman in the Rumble in the Jungle in Zaire.

December 11, 1981
Ali loses his final fight against Trevor Berbick in the Bahamas and retires from boxing for good.

November 19, 1986
Ali marries his fourth and current wife, Lonnie Williams.

November 19, 2005
The Muhammad Ali Center, an $80-million project dedicated to Ali and world peace, opens in the heart of downtown Louisville, Kentucky.

King of the World

I am the king! I am the king! King of the world!

On February 25, 1964, a rumor spread through the steamy streets of Miami. That night, the young boxer Cassius Clay was to fight the Heavyweight champion of the world, Sonny Liston. Clay had been acting strangely, and rumor had it he was at the airport, scrambling to buy a plane ticket out of town. Some believed Clay had lost his mind, others thought he was scared senseless. They all agreed, though, that this loudmouth from Louisville didn't stand a chance against Liston.

Clay, however, didn't just show up for the fight. He dominated it. He danced circles around the champ. Floating like a butterfly *and* stinging like a bee, Clay's lightning-fast punches dazed Liston and dazzled the crowd.

By the end of the sixth **round**, Liston had taken enough abuse. The match was over, and Clay—who would soon change his name to Muhammad Ali—was the new world champion.

Against overwhelming odds, Clay shocked the world. With arms raised, he danced around the ring, howling out words that would soon ring surprisingly true.

"I am the king! I am the king! King of the world!"

This is the story of the reign of Muhammad Ali, who became a world champion boxer and so much more.

CHAPTER 1

The Louisville Lip

His mind was like a March wind, blowing every which way. And whenever I thought I could predict what he'd do, he turned around and proved me wrong.

—*Odessa Clay*

Cassius Marcellus Clay, Jr.—known to the world later in life as Muhammad Ali—was born in Louisville, Kentucky, on January 17, 1942. It was a hectic time in the country. Only a month earlier, Japanese warplanes had launched a surprise attack on American naval forces at Pearl Harbor in Hawaii. While the young boy's proud parents—Cassius Sr. and Odessa—brought their first child home from Louisville General Hospital, the rest of the

country was gearing up to fight World War II.

The Clay name has a long history in Kentucky, and the legend of Cassius Marcellus Clay begins much earlier than

Kentucky's Cassius Marcellus Clay (pictured) spoke out against slavery in the days before the American Civil War.

World War II. Indeed, to understand the story of one of the world's most famous athletes, one needs to travel back two centuries to before another devastating conflict—the American Civil War.

Born in Kentucky in 1810, the first Cassius Marcellus Clay was the white son of a wealthy slaveholder. Early on in his life, this Clay viewed slavery as a great evil, and he soon became an outspoken **abolitionist**. His antislavery views were far from popular in Kentucky, and Clay paid a steep price for speaking out against slavery in his newspaper. Clay not only was beaten by mobs and forced to move several times, but proslavery forces also killed his son. President Abraham Lincoln thought highly of the brave Clay, sending him to Russia to serve as the U.S. **ambassador** in 1861.

Lincoln's Emancipation Proclamation in 1863 freed slaves during the Civil War. Free, if not yet equal, some of the Clay family's former slaves held onto the Clay name to honor Cassius Marcellus Clay's antislavery legacy. Several generations later, the future Heavyweight champion of the world was born and given the name of Cassius Marcellus Clay. Like his namesake, the future boxer would prove to be

This c. 1888 lithograph displays the text of the Emancipation Proclamation, which was an executive order of President Abraham Lincoln that freed slaves in the Confederate states during the American Civil War. After the war ended in 1865, the 13th Amendment officially abolished slavery.

brave and outspoken. And he, too, would learn to pay dearly for voicing his unpopular opinions.

West End Kids

Cassius and his younger brother Rudolph, who was born in 1944, grew up on Grand Street in Louisville's West End neighborhood. A middle-class African American neighborhood, Grand was lined with the homes of hardworking families, and the Clay family at number 3302 was no different. A skilled painter, Cassius Sr. worked mainly on billboards and signs, but occasionally he was able to show off his talents by painting murals in local churches. He made enough money to buy the house they lived in for $4,500—around $55,000 in modern-day dollars. Clay's mother Odessa would sometimes leave the house to cook and clean for Louisville's rich white families. However, she spent most of her time keeping her family home tidy and raising two energetic sons.

As a baby, Cassius displayed some of the same personality for which he would become famous years later. He was only a few months old when he was already trying to talk. Odessa began calling him "G.G." due to sounds he made while babbling constantly. Later, when Clay became a Golden Glove amateur boxing champion, he would tell his mother he had been just trying to say the words, "Golden Gloves." A bundle of energy, Clay rarely sat still. "He was in bed with me at six months, and you know how babies stretch? He had little muscle arms and he hit me in the mouth when he stretched and it loosened my front tooth," Odessa told one interviewer. "I always say his first knockout punch was in my mouth."

Sweet, and with a freckled face, Odessa was a caring and charitable woman. According to Clay, "She taught us to love people and treat everybody with kindness." While Clay idolized his mother, there were times when he feared his father. Loud and barrel-chested, Cassius Sr. was famous in the neighborhood for his amusing impressions of famous singers and his storytelling skills. When mixed with alcohol, however, his prideful personality caused trouble. On several occasions Odessa had to call police officers to remove a drunken Cassius Sr. from the home; and at other

While Clay idolized his mother, there were times when he feared his father.

times, he was arrested for drunk driving and getting into fights. Witnessing how alcohol could transform his father so violently, Clay vowed to never drink alcohol in his life—a promise that he kept.

Even though he had a dark side, Cassius Sr. worked hard with Odessa to instill a sense of pride and responsibility in their sons. On Sundays, Odessa would take the boys to the local Baptist church. And from time to time, the brothers would tag along with their dad to help paint signs. Yet, the brothers still had plenty of time to be boys, playing games, watching television, and hanging out with other kids in the neighborhood. Nearby family members called Cassius and Rudolph the "Wrecking Crew" because whenever they came over, something was bound to get broken. They weren't troublesome kids, just incredibly active, and when they were wrestling or playing catch with a football, things such as birdbaths and windows would often get in the way.

A confident child, Clay was a natural leader, even among older children. "I'd come home and he'd have about fifty boys on the porch—this was when he was about eight years old—

Cassius Clay (right) and his younger brother, Rudolph, were an energetic duo. This photograph shows a teenaged Cassius working out in the gym with help from Rudolph.

and he's talking to all of 'em," Cassius Sr. once said. "A whole neighborhood of boys, and he'd be doing all the talking."

The Color Line

Clay may have been well fed and well loved growing up, but he and his family were still second-class citizens in Louisville for one simple reason—the color of their skin. Through Clay's teenage years, his home state of Kentucky, as well as nearby states, continued to maintain Jim Crow laws **segregating** whites and blacks. The Louisville of Clay's childhood had different stores, restaurants, and even drinking fountains for different

Jim Crow

After the Civil War the brutal practce of slavery was finally brought to an end. Many states both in the North and South, however, were unwilling to treat freed blacks as equals. The states passed what came to be known as Jim Crow laws. Starting in 1876, the purpose of these local and state laws was to give black Americans and other minorities "separate-but-equal" status. Things were far from equal, however.

Jim Crow laws varied from state to state, but common ones banned marriage between different races, forced blacks to sit apart from whites in public places, and required separate schools and libraries for blacks and whites. In some states, Jim Crow laws even created different entrances at hospitals and separate cemeteries for different races. Supporters of the laws claimed that blacks received the same rights and services as whites. In reality, the humiliating Jim Crow regulations made sure blacks received inferior services and treatment. The last of the Jim Crow laws were done away with by 1965, but by then Clay had lived twenty years in a country that legally treated him like a lesser class of human being.

This is the Supreme Court decision in the landmark case of *Plessy v. Ferguson* in 1896. The decision ruled that "separate-but-equal" accommodations were constitutional, resulting in Jim Crow laws in the South. The reality, of course, was that "separate" was not "equal."

Young Cassius and his mom were very close. He gives her a kiss in this photo from 1963.

races. When Clay went to see a movie, he had to sit in the balcony while white people were given the better seats below.

The Clays were a proud family, and for the most part they responded to the cruel laws with dignity. Cassius Sr. and Odessa weren't the only family role models for Clay. He had aunts and uncles nearby who worked hard, saved their money, and lived solid, decent lives. Clay and his brother learned at a young age where they could and couldn't go in town, and they were never physically attacked. Rarely, however, could they forget that they were blacks living in a white person's world. According to Rudolph Clay, "If we were in the wrong place, white boys would come up in a car and . . . tell us to get out if they thought we were someplace we didn't belong."

One tragic incident that did much to remind young Clay of his place in American society was the murder of Emmett Till. Till was a fourteen-year-old black teenager from Chicago, Illinois, who had traveled south in August 1955 to stay with family in Money, Mississippi. Only a few days after arriving, Till was bragging to some friends that he was dating a white girl. He said it loud enough for some nearby whites to overhear. Later on, his friends dared him to say "Hey, baby" to a white woman working in the town.

Till was from Chicago, which had a more relaxed racial atmosphere. He didn't think the dare was that big of a deal. It was a big deal in Mississippi, though, and soon afterward the town was buzzing with news of Till's actions. A few nights later, Till was kidnapped, brutally beaten, and then shot at close range before being thrown into a river. After his body was found, Till's mother let graphic images of her murdered son be taken and printed in newspapers across the country, so that everyone could see how terribly her boy died. Cassius Sr. made sure both of his sons saw the pictures, and the brutal images were burned deep into Cassius's memory.

Equally unforgettable—though sadly unsurprising—to the Clay family was that the white men on trial for the murder of Emmett Till were found not guilty soon after. They were set free to walk the streets again by an all-white jury.

This photo of Emmett Till and his mother was taken c. 1950. The images of Emmett's murder in 1955 left a lasting impression on Cassius.

CHAPTER 2

Good as Gold

To make America the greatest is my goal.

The October day in 1954 that would change the course of twelve-year-old Cassius Clay's life forever started the same as many days before. Clay was horsing around with a neighborhood friend when they decided to check out the Louisville Home Show, an annual fair for black businesses held inside the Columbia Auditorium downtown. To get there, Clay rode his beloved red-and-white Schwinn bicycle—a birthday present received from his parents earlier in the year. After Clay parked his bike outside, the two friends toured the show, filling themselves with the free popcorn and hot dogs being handed out at the various booths. When they left the show to go home, Clay couldn't find his bike. As tears filled his eyes, Clay realized his bike had been stolen.

Never one to sit still, Clay stormed around the auditorium looking for either the bike or the thief. After being told there was a police officer in the basement that might be able to help, Clay marched downstairs to investigate. The officer's name was Joe Martin, and he was busy in an underground gym teaching young men how to box. Standing amid the gym's punching bags and jump-roping fighters, Martin patiently listened to the angry youngster as he complained about the stolen bike. "He was having a fit, half crying because someone stole his bike. He was only twelve years old then, and he said was gonna whup whoever stole it,' Martin recalled. "And I brought up the subject, I said, 'Well, you better learn how to fight before you start challenging people that you're gonna whup.'"

Like a rocket waiting to be launched, that was all the motivation Clay needed to take up boxing. If he ever ran into that thief, Clay knew his boxing skills would make sure the thief never even looked at a red-and-white Schwinn again.

With his parents' go-ahead, Clay immediately began training at Martin's Columbia Gym. The grueling workouts proved to be a perfect outlet for the young boy's near-limitless energy. After six weeks of training, the 85-pound Clay entered the ring to fight his first **bout** against an

Clay was only 12 years old and weighed 85 pounds when he posed for this picture before the first boxing match of his career. The future champion won the fight.

89-pound kid named Ronnie O'Keefe. After winning the majority of the judges' votes in a three-round **split decision**, Clay shouted out that he was going to be "the greatest of all time."

Nobody else in the gym thought so Throughout Clay's first few months of training, Martin considered him to be just an average boxer. As the days piled on top of one another, however, Martin's mind began to change. Never before had he had such a hard worker in his gym. From the start, Clay woke as early as

4:00 a.m. to run several miles in heavy steel-toed work boots before school. He trained at the gym every afternoon, staying long after others his age had gone home. Martin began to sense something special in young Clay. "I realized it was almost impossible to discourage him. He was easily the hardest worker of any kid I ever taught."

The more Clay trained, the more he learned about the art of boxing. His style was unique, his speed was his greatest defense. Even in his early **novice** fights, Clay would quickly step backward to avoid punches rather than block them, which gave him an opening to punch back. Martin did more than train boxers in the gym. He also produced a local television show called *Tomorrow's Champions* that featured young boxers in his gym. Soon enough, Clay was showing off his speedy style in televised matches on Saturday

Boxers wear gloves like the ones shown in this photograph. These cushioned gloves protect the hands of boxers when they fight.

afternoons. By the age of fifteen, he was starting to gain some fame locally. To absolutely nobody's surprise, he loved every moment of it.

The High School Years

Clay entered Louisville's all-black Central High as a tenth-grader in 1957. Right away, the lean yet muscular student stood out in a crowd. Instead of riding a bus to school, Clay jogged for twenty blocks on Chestnut Street alongside it, waving to his fellow classmates as he ran. Although a gifted athlete,

Clay rejected the requests of coaches to play football and other team sports. While some of his teenaged friends began to get into trouble, Clay steadfastly refused to do anything that could jeopardize his future career. "I trained six days a week and never drank or smoked a cigarette. . . . Boxing kept me out of trouble," he said later in life. Clay also created a bizarre energy-packed diet for himself that included a glass of milk with two raw eggs in it for breakfast. He wouldn't even drink soda. Instead, he sipped from a jug of water loaded with fresh garlic, which he claimed kept his blood pressure down.

Clay wasn't a very gifted student, and much of his time in class was spent doodling and daydreaming about boxing matches and future glory. Luckily, school principal Atwood Wilson was impressed both by Clay's dedication to boxing and his gentle nature outside of the ring. Wilson would get on the school intercom and warn

While some of his teenaged friends began to get into trouble, Clay steadfastly refused to do anything that could jeopardize his future career.

students that he'd set Clay on any kids that acted up. At school assemblies, the principal loved to introduce the young boxer as the "next Heavyweight champion of the world." Heavyweight is the top level of the classes of boxing.

Clay was doing everything he could in the ring to prove his principal right. Throughout high school, he drove with his coach, Martin, as far as New York City and San Francisco to compete in **amateur** tournaments—tournaments that, more often than not, he would win. The name Cassius Clay started popping up in boxing conversation more and more often, and not just thanks to his obvious skills in the ring. Clay caused a commotion and even angered some people just about everywhere he went with his energy and motor mouth, taunting his opponents, and sometimes, even their managers. By the age of eighteen, Clay's amateur record was an impressive 100 wins against only 8 losses. And in 1959 and 1960, he won back-to-back national Golden Gloves championships and National Amateur Athletic Union (AAU) titles.

When he wasn't on the road fighting amateur bouts, Clay was pretty easy to find. While continuing to train at Martin's gym, he also worked with boxing trainer Fred Stoner and his all-black team at the Grace Community Center. In addition, before sunrise or after sunset, Clay jogged along the streets of Louisville, bragging to whomever would listen that he was going to be the greatest. Chickasaw Park, the only park in the area that blacks were free to use, was one of his favorite training spots. The folks who hung out at the park quickly got used to hearing Clay's boasts on a daily basis. "Cassius Clay used to come up the street acting like he was hitting people, shadowboxing and throwing punches," Louisville native Lawrence McKinley recalls. "Nobody ever dreamed he'd be world champ."

With a little help from Principal Wilson, Clay graduated in 1960. Academically he was ranked only 376 out of 391 students. But as he walked up to get his diploma, his fellow students showed how much they cared for Clay by giving him a standing ovation.

An Olympic Spirit

As an amateur boxer, Clay had one last goal to check off his list: an Olympic gold medal. The Summer Olympic Games in 1960 were held in Rome, Italy, but before Clay could make the trip, he had to make the team. The Olympic trials were

Golden Gloves

One of the greatest honors an amateur boxer can win is a Golden Gloves trophy. Started in 1923 by *Chicago Tribune* sports editor Arch Ward, the Golden Gloves began as a citywide amateur boxing tournament. The champion in each weight class was awarded a miniature golden boxing glove, which gave the tournament its name. The tournament quickly spread to other major cities, such as New York, Detroit, and St. Louis; and soon the champions from various states and even other countries began competing in larger tournaments to declare overall champions. Past Golden Gloves greats include boxing legends such as Joe Louis, Sugar Ray Leonard, Tommy Hearns, Evander Holyfield, Oscar De La Hoya, and, of course, Cassius Clay (Muhammad Ali).

Several boxing champions got their start as Golden Gloves winners. Among them was the legendary Joe Louis (pictured). In the 1930s and 1940s, the "Brown Bomber" held the Heavyweight title longer than anyone else before or since.

at the Cow Palace in San Francisco, California, and Clay (as usual) spent a great deal of his time inside and outside of the ring bragging about his skills. Unhappy with the cocky boxer, the crowd booed Clay as he entered the ring to face off against the U.S. Army's top Light heavyweight boxer, Allen Hudson. The first two rounds of the three-round bout were evenly matched, but Clay ended the fight in the third with a series of devastating punches. The 178-pound, eighteen-year-old Clay became the U.S. Olympic boxing team's official entry in the Light heavyweight division. (Boxing matchups are determined by the weight of the fighters.)

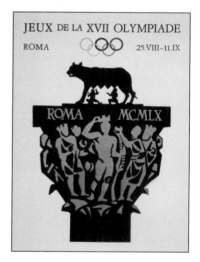

This is a commemorative poster from the 1960 Olympic Games. At 18, Clay headed to the Games in Rome, Italy, as a Light heavyweight boxer.

Winning a spot on the Olympic team proved to be the easy part. The tougher part was actually getting to Rome. Clay may have spent the past few years crisscrossing the country, but he had always traveled by car, bus, or train. The big, bad boxer was afraid of few things, but he was absolutely terrified of flying. At first Clay refused to even consider stepping foot on an airplane, claiming he could take a boat to Italy. Coach Martin had to spend hours calming Clay down and convincing him that if he ever wanted to become a world champion, he had to first fly to Italy. Clay eventually agreed but never felt good about it. In fact, on the entire plane ride to Rome, Clay wore a parachute that he'd purchased at an army surplus store!

How Cassius Took Rome

From almost the first time he stepped into the ring, Clay loved making up rhymes about how great he was—and how bad his opponents were. The following is Clay's first published poem, read to an adoring crowd upon his victorious return to Louisville after the Olympics.

How Cassius Took Rome

To make America the greatest is my goal,
So I beat the Russian, and I beat the Pole,
And for the USA won the Medal of Gold.
Italians said, "You're greater than the Cassius of Old.
We like your name, we like your game,
So make Rome your home if you will."
I said I appreciated your kind hospitality,
But the USA is my country still,
'Cause they waiting to welcome me in Louisville.

After touching down in Italy, Clay got to work meeting athletes from around the world. Just as he had in high school, Clay quickly made his presence felt. Smiling and joking with everyone he ran into, he soon was nicknamed the Mayor of Olympic Village. If anything, Clay trained harder in Italy than he had before. His roommate at the Olympics, fellow U.S. boxer Wilbert McClure, remembers that "we'd walk around and he'd go up to people and shake hands with them, but he had his mind on training . . . he was one of the hardest trainers I ever saw."

In the ring, it was business as usual as Clay darted and danced to win his first two matches. His third match was against

Australian Tony Madigan, whom Clay had beaten a year earlier at a Chicago Golden Gloves event. Once again, Clay walked away with the victory.

It was then time for the gold-medal match against Poland's Zbigniew Pietrzykowski. A left-hander, the Polish champion had won a bronze medal at the Olympics four years earlier and was a three-time European champion. For the first half of the fight, Clay was dazed by Pietrzykowski's tricky left-handed stance, and the American took too many punches. Something clicked in the middle of the second round, however, and Clay started landing hard punches. Clay knew that to win the gold, he'd have to have a huge final round. He stormed out of his corner in the third round with sharp punches and expert footwork. By the time the bell rang to end the fight, Pietrzykowski was slumped against the ropes. Only six years after he'd first picked up a pair of boxing gloves, Clay was able to raise his arms in the ring as an Olympic champion.

Afterward, Clay refused to take off his gold medal, even wearing it when he went to bed at night. Following a quick stop in New York City, he returned to Louisville for a heroic homecoming. Twenty police cars met him at the

As the gold-medal winner, Clay stands on the highest step at his boxing class's awards presentation at the 1960 Olympics. The silver medal winner, Zbigniew Pietrzykowski, stands at the right, while bronze medalists Tony Madigan and Giulio Saraudi are at the left.

airport and escorted him back to a pep rally at his former high school. Near a banner reading "Welcome Home Champ," the mayor of Louisville gave a speech in which he told Clay he was "a credit to Louisville . . . [and] an inspiration to the young people of this city."

Unfortunately, not everyone in the city agreed with the mayor. Only days after the parade in his honor, Clay was refused entry into a restaurant because he was black. Even after winning a gold medal for his country, Clay continued to be treated as a lesser citizen.

Clay was driven through the Louisville streets in a parade in his honor after winning a gold medal at the 1960 Olympics. But that didn't change the way businesses treated black customers.

CHAPTER 3

A Brash Beginning

All he wanted to do was train and fight, train and fight.
        —*Angelo Dundee*

With an Olympic gold medal around his neck, Cassius Clay had accomplished everything he could as an amateur boxer. He had nowhere to go but pro. Clay could start making some of his dreams come true, earning enough to buy his parents a new house. He could also buy a shiny new Cadillac car for himself, just like the one his boxing idol Sugar Ray Robinson drove.

By now, knowledge of Clay's talents had traveled well beyond Louisville. Clay did much to spread the word on his own, talking to reporters and ordinary people before, after, and during the Olympic Games. When Wilma Rudolph, one of Clay's Olympic teammates and a three-time

Cassius sits with his mother, Odessa, in his Cadillac in front of their Louisville home. By turning pro, he made enough money to buy himself a new car and his parents a new house.

gold medalist in track, came to visit him in Louisville after the Games, he drove her around in a convertible yelling out, "I'm Cassius Clay! I am the greatest!" to everyone they passed.

Clay, though, needed financial help to turn pro as boxers early in their career make very little money. A long list of wealthy people from across the country lined up to **sponsor** the young boxer, each promising to lead him to the Heavyweight world championship. With his father's approval, Clay signed on with a set known as the Louisville Sponsoring Group. Made up of eleven wealthy white men from the area that came together to guide and invest in Clay, the group supplied the young boxer with the funds and training he needed to go pro, including a $10,000 signing bonus plus $300 a month in earnings to begin his training. In exchange for their risk in supporting a boxer who had yet to earn anything in the ring, they were to receive a percentage of Clay's professional earnings.

Only three days after signing with the Louisville Sponsoring Group, Clay made his professional boxing debut. On October 29, 1960, he fought a part-time boxer and full-time police chief named Tunney Hunsaker. Hansaker recalled years later that Clay "was fast as lightning and he could hit from any position without getting hit. I tried every trick I knew to throw him off balance, but he was just too good."

While happy with the victory, Clay and his sponsors knew the competition was only going to become harder. It was time for Clay to study with an experienced trainer. In November, Clay went to California to work with Archie Moore, the Light heavyweight champion who continued to fight at the age of forty-seven. Moore's dusty training camp near San Diego, nicknamed the Salt Mine, was dotted with huge boulders that had the names of great fighters painted on them. The boulders

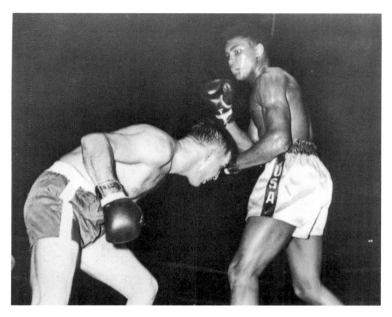

Clay's first professional fight came in Louisville against Tunney Hunsaker (left). Hunsaker, the chief of police in Fayetteville, West Virginia, was no match for Clay.

and rough-and-tumble gym awed Clay from the moment he arrived. "I'm gonna get a camp like this some day," he promised.

The two men respected each other, and Moore was impressed with Clay's raw talent and dedication to training. Clay, however, wasn't a fan of Moore's training rules. Clay couldn't stand doing his share of daily chores, part of every fighter's responsibilities at the camp. The Louisville Lip, as Clay was nicknamed thanks to his motor mouth, frequently complained that he didn't come to the Salt Mine to learn to wash dishes. And he didn't like Moore's advice in the ring, either. The older boxer wanted Clay to quit ducking and dancing so much, and instead focus on learning knockout punches that could end fights quickly. Moore, who had been boxing professionally since 1938 and would fight

Boxing Rules

Unlike those of team sports such as baseball and football, the rules of boxing are pretty simple. Two boxers—also known as pugilists—enter the ring to fight between three and fifteen rounds. Each round lasts three minutes, and there is a one-minute break between them, during which the boxers return to a corner of the ring to get advice and treatment from their trainers. A referee in the ring controls the fight, making sure the boxers don't throw illegal punches and that they follow the basic rules. The referee is also there to count out boxers who have been knocked down. If a boxer can't stand up after a ten-second count, the other boxer wins by a knockout (also known as a KO). If the referee decides a boxer is too hurt to continue fighting, then the other boxer wins by a technical knockout (also known as a TKO). Outside of the ring, judges score the fight round by round, paying attention to which boxer lands the most punches and knockdowns (meaning a boxer is hit and falls to the floor of the ring but gets up quickly). If neither boxer is knocked out of the fight, it's up to the judges to decide the winner. A unanimous decision means all the judges agree on the winner; a split decision means at least one of the judges gave the losing boxer higher scores. A draw is a tie, meaning neither boxer wins or loses.

more than 200 times in his career, knew Clay could last longer as a boxer by ending fights quickly and taking fewer punches. However, Clay, who dreamed of being a flashy fighter who retired young, enjoyed this advice about as much as he enjoyed scrubbing dishes.

In early December, Clay left the camp to visit his family for the holidays. Both men knew he wasn't going to return.

Miami Heat

In need of a new trainer for its young boxer, the Louisville Sponsoring Group figured Miami-based Angelo Dundee would be a good fit. Dundee turned out to be the group's finest decision, staying on as Clay's trusted trainer throughout his entire career.

Clay had already met the highly respected Dundee several times before in Louisville, having visited the trainer when Dundee brought some of his boxers into town. This time, Clay had to go to Dundee, which meant moving to Miami. Clay was so excited he left Louisville before Christmas in 1960 to begin a new life in southern Florida.

Dundee's facility, the Fifth Street Gym, was far from pretty. In fact, it was a

Clay began training with Angelo Dundee late in 1960. The two men, seen here in 1962, worked together for the rest of the boxer's career.

downright ugly place, infested with rats and lit by bare lightbulbs hanging low over a plywood floor. But that hadn't stopped the talented Dundee from training several champion boxers in the gym.

Clay and Dundee were a perfect team. Unlike Archie Moore, Dundee didn't try to mold Clay into a different kind of boxer.

Instead, he let Clay be himself, changing what he didn't like about the boxer's technique through positive reinforcement and simple suggestions. In return, Clay trained harder than any boxer Dundee had ever seen. "[He] never complained about nothing. All he wanted to do was train and fight, train and fight."

And Clay thrived under Dundee's laid-back style. "Angelo Dundee was with me from my second professional fight.

Dundee's facility, the Fifth Street Gym, was far from pretty. In fact, it was a downright ugly place, infested with rats and lit by bare lightbulbs . . .

And no matter what happened after that, he was always my friend," the champ would say years later. "There was no bossing, no telling me what to do and not do, in or out of the ring. He was just there when I needed him, and he always treated me with respect. There just wasn't any problem ever between us."

With Dundee by his side, Clay began to transform from a fit teenager into a muscle-bound man. By the middle of February 1961, Clay had won four more professional fights, all by knockout. Clay was winning his fights, but the local boxing crowd remained unimpressed. Many boxing writers and fans couldn't see past Clay's big mouth, claiming that his bark was far worse than his bite.

That belief began to change when former Heavyweight champion Ingemar Johansson came to Miami for a rematch against the current titleholder, Floyd Patterson. Clay managed to get into Johansson's camp as a **sparring partner**, and quickly embarrassed the slower Swedish star by circling him and peppering him with lightning fast **jabs**, all while saying things

Angelo Dundee

In 1921, Angelo Dundee became the fifth of seven children born into a family of illiterate Italian immigrants living in Philadelphia. He began his career as boxing trainer and **cornerman** at the famed Stillman's Gym in New York City in the 1940s, starting as a simple "bucketman." As a bucketman, his responsibilities included sweeping the gym, making sure boxers had plenty of water, and holding out a bucket for fighters to spit into during fights. Well-liked by just about everyone he met, Dundee spent his time at the gym watching how the older trainers worked the fighters. They gave fighters advice on how to box and kept them in shape. But Dundee also noticed how trainers filled fighters with confidence, pushing them to be their best.

When his brother Chris, a boxing promoter himself, moved to Miami to open a gym, he had Angelo join him as the head trainer. Dundee soon was managing a stable of top fighters, including champions Sugar Ramos and Luis Rodriguez. But it was the arrival of Cassius Clay in late 1960 that brought Dundee his greatest success, a partnership that would last for more than two decades. Dundee was immediately impressed by Clay: "Training him was a whole different ball game from most fighters. You didn't have to push. It was like jet [power]. Just touch him and he took off."

like, "I'm the one who should be fighting Patterson, not you!" and, "What's the matter? Can't you catch me?" An exhausted Johansson stopped sparring Clay after only two rounds and everyone in the gym knew that Clay—who was only nineteen-years-old—was the better boxer.

Knockout Predictions

Realizing Clay was ready for a stiffer challenge, Dundee pitted him against Lamar Clark, a talented boxer with a mighty knockout punch. Speaking to the press before the fight, Clay predicted he would knock out the more experienced Clark in the second round. Fighting in his hometown of Louisville on April 19, a pumped-up Clay charged out swinging hard and fast. Clark had dozens of professional wins on his side, but that was no match for Clay's shocking speed and snappy punches. After breaking Clark's nose, Clay knocked him out in the second round—just as he had promised.

When nineteen-year-old Clay traveled to Las Vegas, Nevada, for his seventh professional fight, he'd already earned a lifetime's worth of nicknames. Most—such as "Claptrap Clay" and "Mighty Mouth"—were based on his nonstop bragging. But during a radio interview in Las Vegas, Clay met a man who made the Louisville Lip seem as quiet as a librarian. Nearly fifty years old, "Gorgeous" George Wagner was a professional wrestler famed for his big blond hair and even bigger mouth. After Clay's

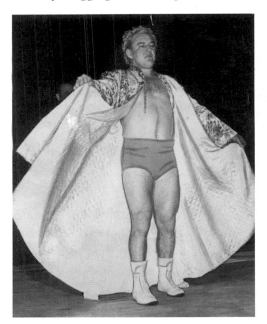

Wrestler Gorgeous George was a flamboyant personality who influenced Clay's decision to become more of a showman.

interview ended, he watched Gorgeous George shouting that if he lost his next fight, he'd cut off all his hair. Of course, Gorgeous George continued, that could never happen because his opponent was a bum and he was the "greatest wrestler in the world!" After the show, George gave Clay some advice that stayed with the boxer throughout his career: "A lot of people will pay to see someone [try to] shut your mouth." Clay decided then and there to kick his mouthing off up a notch: "I'd never been shy about talking, but if I talked even more, there was no telling how much money people would pay to see me."

Clay's fight in Las Vegas was against a gigantic Hawaiian boxer named Duke Sabedong. It was Clay's toughest fight yet, and Sabedong managed to stay in the ring for a full fifteen rounds. Still, Clay left the ring with another win and a perfect 7–0 record. Afterward, Clay's fame grew at a faster pace, and his fights began to be aired on television—a rare honor for such a young boxer. Clay returned the favor by continuing to predict when each of his battles would end. "No one shut him up" by beating him, explained Ferdie Pacheco, Clay's fight doctor. "And so he just kept predicting and winning, predicting and winning."

Throughout 1961 and 1962, Clay mowed down a steady stream of better and better boxers. At 9–0, Clay was matched against a boxer named Willie Besmanoff. Before the fight, Clay spoke to the press. "I'm embarrassed to get in the ring with this unrated duck. I'm ready for top contenders like Patterson and Sonny Liston. Besmanoff must fall in seven." During the fight, Clay toyed with Besmanoff to keep him around long enough for the seventh round. And when that round came up, Clay promptly knocked him out.

At 15–0, Clay was scheduled to fight his biggest bout yet against his former trainer, Archie Moore, in Los Angeles. To promote the fight on November 15, 1962, the two boxers traded boasts and dares. "When you come to the fight, don't block the aisle and don't block the door/You will all go home after round four," Clay rhymed, predicting the fight would end in the fourth round. Moore, a showman himself, responded: "The only way I fall in four is by toppling over Clay's prostrate [lying down] form."

In reality, the fight wasn't very fair. The fifty-year-old Moore tired quickly as Clay danced circles around him, landing almost every punch he threw. When the bell rang to begin the fourth round, Clay came out swinging even harder, soon tagging Moore

Before a fight on November 15, 1962, Clay boldly wrote on a chalkboard that he would knock out Archie Moore in the fourth round—he predicted right.

with a vicious **uppercut**. A few punches later, Moore was flat on his back. Yet, before the count of ten, the woozy Moore managed to rise long enough to receive a second batch of punches. The fight was over, and the crowd did indeed "all go home after round four."

London Calling

Two fights after beating Moore, Clay went toe-to-toe against Doug Jones at New York City's Madison Square Garden. It was an off night for Clay, who predicted a knockout in the sixth round. Instead, the judges awarded him an uninspired victory after ten rounds, and the unhappy crowd booed Clay's boring performance as he left the stadium.

To get back in the spotlight, Clay traveled to London, England, three months later to fight the British champion Henry Cooper on June 18, 1963. The fight, which was held in Wembley Stadium, attracted 55,000 people. Most were there to cheer for Cooper, their countryman. Having predicted he'd knock Cooper out in the fifth round, Clay entered the ring wearing a crown and a red robe with "Cassius the Greatest" written on the back. For the first few rounds, Clay was indeed great. By round three, the Englishman was bleeding and ready to fall. Clay, though, seemed to want to keep his promise of a fifth-round knockout. He paid dearly for his cockiness, as in the fourth round Cooper landed his mighty left **hook**—nicknamed Henry's Hammer—square onto Clay's chin. Clay managed to woozily stand as the round ended. but he was in big trouble.

To revive Clay, his cornermen rubbed ice on his back and had him sniff **smelling salts**. Dundee knew Clay needed more time to clear his head. A quick thinker, Dundee requested that the referee come over and inspect a tear in Clay's glove that he had noticed earlier. The referee gave Clay's corner extra time to tape up the glove, time Clay needed to clear his muddled mind. "I don't know how much time that got us," Dundee later said. "Maybe a minute, but it was enough." Feeling revived, Clay started the fifth round with a brutal flurry of punches that lasted nearly two full minutes. The referee finally stepped in to award Clay the TKO and to save Cooper from any more abuse. Clay's prefight prediction had again come true.

After the bout, Clay grew even bolder. "I'm not the greatest. I'm the double greatest. Not only do I knock 'em out, I pick the round," he told reporters. "I'm the boldest, the prettiest, the most superior, most scientific, most skillfullest

Clay was in trouble against Britain's Herry Cooper (pictured) in their 1963 fight, but rallied, leading to a fifth-round TKO to fulfill another prediction.

fighter in the ring today." Now, with a perfect professional record of 19–0, Clay's big mouth was becoming impossible to ignore. It's not bragging, the old sports saying goes, if you can back it up.

CHAPTER 4

A King Is Crowned

Float like a butterfly, sting like a bee.

On September 25, 1962, Sonny Liston became the world Heavyweight champion by knocking out Floyd Patterson. He needed only two minutes and six seconds to pummel Patterson into submission. Ten months later, Sonny squared off against Patterson once again. This time, he needed a little more time—four additional seconds, to be exact—to knock out the former champion. With these impressive wins behind him, experts were beginning to agree that Liston might be the best Heavyweight champion of all time. Nobody ever argued that he was also one of the scariest.

Years later, Cassius Clay would admit that he, too, was afraid of the mighty Liston. At the time, he did a good job of hiding those fears, daring Liston to a fight each time they crossed paths. The up-and-coming Clay was in the audience at each of the Liston/Patterson fights, making his presence known at both. Patterson barely had time to get up

Sonny Liston (standing) pounded former Heavyweight champion Floyd Patterson twice before fighting Clay.

after his second loss before Clay was in the ring, screaming to all who would listen. "That fight was a disgrace! Liston is a tramp! I'm the champ." Police officers had to hold Clay back as he ran toward Liston, hollering, "Don't make me wait! I'll whup him in eight!"

Many boxing writers and fans found Clay's clowning around to be rude and disrespectful. He should just zip his lip and box, some said. Others thought he wasn't paying enough respect to those above him. Although Clay had been winning his fights handily, crowds began booing the cocky young man whenever he made an appearance.

To Liston, Clay seemed like little more than an irritating little brother or even a fly buzzing around his head. Sure, all the noise Clay made could be annoying. However, all it would take to get rid of him would be a quick swat or two. Figuring that a fight with the loudmouth would be both easy and a rewarding payday, Liston signed on to fight Clay on February 25, 1964. The Louisville Sponsoring Group didn't think Clay was ready for such a challenge, and virtually all the experts figured he'd be beaten easily. Clay, however, had a plan. Plus, he wouldn't have very far to travel to take on Liston and his daunting 36–1 record. The fight was to take place in Miami.

Training for Trouble

Before the fight in Miami, Dundee's Fifth Street Gym turned into a circus. The public was let in for a small fee to watch Clay train, and magazines around the country sent writers to cover the fight. Clay happily played the part of ringleader, entertaining bystanders with rhymes and bragging about the many ways he was going to beat Liston, whom he kept calling a "big, ugly bear." "I'm going to put that ugly bear on the floor, and after the

Sonny Liston

Charles "Sonny" Liston once said that boxing is like a cowboy movie: "There's got to be good guys and there's got to be bad guys. That's what people pay for—to see the bad guy get beat. So I'm the bad guy. But I change things. I don't get beat."

Liston was the second youngest of thirteen children in a family of poor **sharecroppers** in Arkansas. From the age of eight, he worked in the fields instead of going to school. His father was abusive, and by the time Liston was a teenager, he had run away and was getting into trouble in St. Louis, Missouri. At twenty-two, he was sentenced to five years in prison for armed robbery. While in jail, Liston learned to box. He soon became the prison's Heavyweight champion.

Once out of prison, Liston began boxing professionally. Opponents quickly found out that his punches were as powerful as a freight train. Liston won one memorable fight in only 58 seconds—and when it was over, his foe had seven teeth stuck in his protective mouthpiece. Liston battled on for five troubled years after fighting Clay a second time, ending with an impressive record of fifty wins and four losses. He died in 1971.

Sonny Liston, pictured here, was a powerful puncher who instilled fear in all of his opponents—even Cassius Clay.

fight I'm gonna build myself a pretty home and use him as a bearskin rug," he'd say. Clay acted so confidently that he was also quoted as saying that "if Sonny Liston whups me, I'll kiss his feet in the ring, crawl out of the ring on my knees, tell him he's the greatest, and catch the next jet out of the country."

To help drum up attention for the upcoming fight, the promoters had the Beatles—in town for a television show appearance—stop by the gym. With cameras clicking, Clay goofed around with the famous band, claiming that he was still the greatest but they were the prettiest. While such performances gave journalists plenty to write about, few believed what came out of Clay's mouth. As the day of the fight approached, Clay remained the underdog.

Across town, Liston thought much the same. Unlike Clay, who continued to train hard at Dundee's moldy gym, Liston

The Beatles were among the few personalities that could match Clay's fame in the 1960s—although they couldn't compete with the boxer in this "fight" in 1964.

Clay made a surprise visit to Sonny Liston's training center before their fight in 1964 and showed how he intended to handle the champ.

worked out in the plush Surfside Civic Auditorium. The champion trained only in spurts, barely breaking a sweat. "My only worry is how I'll get my fist outta his big mouth once I get him in the ring," Liston said. "It's gonna go so far down his throat, it'll take a week for me to pull it out again."

Beneath the surface, however, Clay's plan was starting to work. Aware that Liston was a tough and talented boxer, Clay hoped to get Liston so angry he'd forget his boxing skills and instead just try to pound Clay into the ground. Weeks before the fight, Clay and some friends drove a bus all the way to Liston's home in Denver, Colorado, waking up the champion at 2 a.m. and taunting him on his front lawn. Back in Miami, Clay was insulting Liston at every turn, even meeting the champ's flight into the city. Slowly, Clay was getting deeper and deeper under Liston's skin.

Newspapers ran the "Tale of the Tape"—the boxers' physical statistics, as shown here—before Cassius Clay and Sonny Liston squared off in the ring in 1964.

LISTON		CLAY
31	AGE	23
212	WEIGHT	210
	HEIGHT	
6 ft. 1 in.		6 ft. 3 in.
	REACH	
84 in.		79 in.
	CHEST NORMAL	
44 in.		43 in
	CHEST EXPANDED	
46½ in.		45 in.
	WAIST	
33 in.		34 in.
	FOREARM	
14½ in.		13½ in.
	FIST	
15½ in.		13 in.
	NECK	
17½ in.		17¾ in.
	BICEPS	
17½ in.		16 in.

The morning of the fight, Clay put on his biggest performance yet. He arrived at the mandatory weigh-in wearing a denim jacket with the words "Bear Huntin'" stitched in red on it. Upon seeing Liston, Clay seemed to lose control, shaking and yelling that he was ready to rumble. "You ain't no giant! I'm gonna eat you alive," he yelled, lunging toward Liston. Bystanders had to hold Clay back while he and his friend Drew "Bundini" Brown chanted, "Float like a butterfly, sting like a bee." Liston, along with most the crowd, thought Clay had lost his mind. After Clay was fined $2,500 by the Miami Beach Boxing Commission for his outbursts, the fighters weighed in. Clay was a fit 210 pounds, while the shorter but stockier Liston came in at 212 pounds.

An hour later, Clay explained why he had acted so wild. "Because Liston thinks I'm a nut. He is scared of no man, but he is scared of a nut. Now he doesn't know what I'm going to do."

An Unforgettable Upset

That day, a rumor swept through Miami that Clay had been spotted at the airport buying a plane ticket out of town. People figured Clay was so scared of Liston, his only choice was to fly away. Instead, Clay calmly showed up at the arena. "For all the joking and clowning that morning, he knew this was serious business. This was everything he'd every dreamed of, and a very tough customer stood in his way," explained his trainer, Angelo Dundee.

As the opening bell rang for the fight, Clay set out to show Liston what he meant by "float like a butterfly, sting like a bee." With his hands held dangerously low, leaving his face unguarded, a ducking and weaving Clay floated around most of the champ's punches. And as the round wound down, Clay began peppering Liston with jabs and hooks, letting his opponent know he could sting as well. A surprised crowd roared as Clay's punches hit their target.

A shocked Liston came out firing huge blows in Round 2. Circling around the slower brawler, Clay continued to avoid most of the punches and hammered on his opponent. Liston connected with a giant left hook that staggered Clay, but Clay returned the favor by opening a cut under Liston's left eye. In Round 3, the crowd rose to its feet as Clay landed a vicious combination of strikes, causing a wobbly Liston to fall back into the ringside ropes. With Liston's nose bleeding, Clay added insult to injury. "Come on, you bum," he spat out.

With Liston's nose bleeding, Clay added insult to injury. "Come on, you bum," he spat out.

By the fourth round, Clay was in full control, but disaster struck. His eyes began burning furiously, forcing him to blink them shut. To this day, some believe Liston's corner spread an illegal substance on his gloves to blind Clay, while others say it must have been something that accidentally rubbed off the cuts on Liston's face. Whatever the case, Clay was having a lot of trouble seeing clearly. Liston took advantage, landing a powerful left hook. Clay spent most of the next round half-blind and backpedaling, trying to avoid Liston's jabs and punches.

When his vision returned in Round 6, Clay launched punch after punch at an exhausted Liston, landing left-handed jabs followed by explosive right-handed hooks. Dog-tired but never knocked down, Liston sat on his stool at the end of the round and refused to stand for the start of Round 7. Watching Liston spit out his mouthpiece, Clay was one of the first in the arena to realize what was happening. The champion was quitting. The Louisville Lip had won.

Throwing his arms into the air, Clay triumphantly danced around the ring. For once, few felt the need to argue with the words pouring out of the new champion's mouth: "I am the king! I am the king! King of the world!"

"I am the greatest!" Clay shouted to anyone that would listen after his stunning victory over Sonny Liston in 1964.

CHAPTER 5

The Name's Ali, Muhammad Ali

A rooster crows only when it sees the light. Put him in the dark, and he'll never crow. I have seen the light, and I'm crowing.

According to the lessons Cassius Clay learned from wrestler Gorgeous George, his title fight against Sonny Liston in Miami should have been a sold-out victory. For weeks before the fight, Clay drummed up as much excitement as possible, running his mouth nonstop. Still, only half of the seats in the arena were filled for the fight.

This lack of enthusiasm was due in part to Clay's being such an underdog. Why buy a ticket for a fight that would be over in minutes? But there was another reason so few came to the fight, and it had nothing to do with Clay's boxing skills.

For years, there had been hints that Clay, whose family was Christian, was interested in the Nation of Islam. Also known as the Black Muslims, this religious group was very controversial. Led by Elijah Muhammad, the Nation had very different beliefs than others in the Islamic faith around the world. Along with referring to whites as "blue-eyed devils," Muhammad and his followers angered both blacks and whites by teaching that the **integration** of races—one of the main goals of the **civil**

Elijah Muhammad (1898–1975)

Born Elijah Poole in the state of Georgia in 1898, Elijah Muhammad moved to Detroit, Michigan, in the 1920s. There he met W. D. Fard, a man claiming to be a religious prophet. Inspired by Fard's teaching at the Temple of Islam, Muhammad set on a mission to free blacks in America by teaching them to be independent of whites. He lectured that God's true name was Allah and that his true religion was Islam. The Nation of Islam's form of the Islamic religion, however, had plenty of improbable beliefs—including the idea that Earth and the moon were once connected and that aliens in a giant spaceship circled Earth. Muhammad took over as the leader of the Nation of Islam in 1934 and remained the group's head minister until his death in 1975.

Elijah Muhammad, seen here in 1964, was the leader of the Nation of Islam from 1934 until his death in 1975.

rights movement—was unneeded. Blacks could rise to power separately on their own land, they preached.

Before Clay's first fight with Liston, stories circulated that Clay had become a Black Muslim. In the previous year, Clay had attended several public rallies, and one of the group's leaders, Malcolm X, had become one of Clay's close friends. A few weeks before the fight, Clay's father angrily told a reporter that his son had joined the Nation of Islam and that the religious group only wanted his money. Hoping to keep attention on his fight and not on his personal life, Clay refused to answer directly whether he had joined the Nation. All that changed, however, after Liston refused to rise off his stool, making Clay the world Heavyweight champion.

A New Religion, a New Name

At a press conference two days after the fight, Clay announced that he had joined the Nation of Islam. While the news caused a great uproar, it was hardly a surprise to those close to Clay. For years he had shown interest in the Nation of Islam. In high school, Clay had tried to write a report about the group. After moving to Miami, he met a follower of Elijah Muhammad named Captain Sam. "He invited me to a meeting, and after that, my life changed," the champ explained years later. From that point on, Clay attended similar lectures whenever he could.

At the press conference, Clay explained that he could no longer sit quietly as a Christian in a country in which black people were being killed for trying to live equal lives. He said he wasn't a troublemaker and that the Nation of Islam had no plans to take over the country, but he wasn't going to keep his beliefs quiet either. "You can't condemn a man for wanting peace," he said. "A rooster crows only when it sees the light. Put

Clay listens as Elijah Muhammad delivers a speech to Nation of Islam followers in 1964. That was the same year the boxer changed his name to Muhammad Ali.

him in the dark, and he'll never crow I have seen the light, and I'm crowing."

It was hard for most Americans, particularly white Americans, to understand why Clay was so attracted to the Nation of Islam. However, they hadn't been refused service at a restaurant or been made to sit at the back of a bus—even after winning an Olympic gold medal for their country. The group's lectures on black power and pride appealed to Clay, as did their strict rules, which banned drinking and smoking and ordered followers to eat healthily and treat women with respect.

Within a few years, Clay's beliefs would begin to relax and become less severe, but at the time, his views were incredibly radical to most of the country. In addition, boxers at that time were supposed to fight and look good—not necessarily talk or be political—especially if they were black. As any of Clay's high school teachers could have said, though, trying to keep Clay quiet was an impossible task.

In a radio broadcast a few weeks after the Liston fight, Elijah Muhammad announced that Cassius Clay would from then on be known as Muhammad Ali. It was common for members of the Nation of Islam to change names, as they no longer wanted to be linked with the slave owners in their family's past. "Changing my name was one of the most important things that happened to me in my life," Ali told his biographer later in life. "If I had changed my name from Cassius Clay to something like Smith or Jones because I wanted a name that white people thought was more American, nobody would have complained. I was honored that Elijah Muhammad gave me a truly beautiful name." The name *Muhammad* means "worthy of praise," while Ali was the name of a cousin of the Islamic prophet Allah.

Plenty of people did complain about the name change. Days after, Ali was booed while watching a boxing match in New York City. Even though dozens of sports stars and actors had changed their names before, many writers refused to use Ali's new name, continuing to call him Cassius Clay. Feeling like he was under attack by the

> *"Changing my name was one of the most important things that happened to me in my life. . . ."*

press, Ali left the country for a month long tour of Africa. Upon arriving in Ghana, he was treated like a hero. Crowds chanted "Ali, Ali, Ali" wherever he went. The champ—who visited both the pyramids and the president in Egypt—realized just how far his fame had spread.

Muhammad Ali and his brother, who changed his name to Rahaman Ali, get ready to board a plane for Ghana in 1964.

Tagging along with Ali to Africa was Herbert Muhammad, one of Elijah Muhammad's six sons. Herbert would soon become Ali's manager, too. Upon returning to the United States, Herbert introduced Ali to a former beauty-pageant queen named Sonji Roi. Sonji later admitted that Ali asked her to marry him on their very first date, but she couldn't tell if he was kidding or not. If he was, it was only a small joke. The two bonded quickly and were formally married on August 14, 1964, just six weeks after they met.

A Second Dance with Sonny

Around the same time that Ali was married, he agreed to a rematch with Sonny Liston. The fight was scheduled to take place in Boston, Massachusetts, on November 16, 1964. This time, Liston promised, he wouldn't make the same mistake of taking his opponent lightly. Liston trained furiously, getting himself into superb shape. But only three days before the fight, Ali was rushed to the hospital with severe stomach pain. He had to have emergency surgery for a **hernia**, and the rematch was postponed until May 25, 1965.

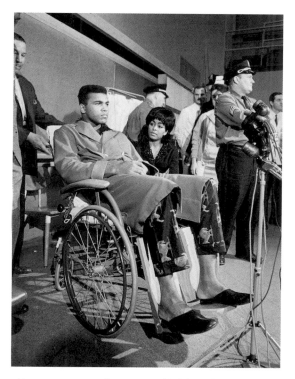

Ali is pictured here at a press conference in a wheelchair after a hernia operation in 1964. Sonji, whom Ali married three months earlier, looks on.

While Ali was recuperating from the surgery, a bitter fight was occurring within the Nation of Islam. Malcolm X, a onetime leader in the group, was kicked out by Elijah Muhammad for publicly discussing the 1963 assassination of President John F. Kennedy. Muhammad didn't want his followers to speak out about the murder, as he feared it would bring more hatred against his group. On February 21, 1965, Malcolm X was assassinated while giving a speech in New York City. On that same night, someone tried to burn down Ali's apartment. Two days later, the Nation of Islam headquarters in New York was bombed. Three members of the Nation of Islam were eventually convicted for the murder of Malcolm X.

Ali's world outside of the ring may have been spinning out of control, but inside of it, he was becoming stronger, faster, and more confident. In fact, Ali's emergency surgery hurt Liston more than it did the champ in the end. Liston had trained his hardest for the fight but then had to wait an additional six months to be in it. Finding it hard to retain his passion of training, Liston showed up for the fight in only decent shape. Ali, however, was as fit as he'd ever been.

Fewer than 3,000 fans showed up for the fight, as it had been moved to tiny Lewiston, Maine. The promoters in Boston had backed out due to all the controversy regarding Ali. Surrounded by Nation of Islam bodyguards, Ali bounced into the ring as a smattering of boos rained down. Liston was cheered heartily when his name was announced.

The crowd didn't get much time to boo Ali or cheer Liston. The fight was over almost before it started. After exchanging a few shots, Ali unleashed what would come to be known as "the phantom

. . . Ali bounced into the ring as a smattering of boos rained down.

Malcolm X

Born Malcolm Little in 1925, Malcolm X first met Muhammad Ali at a Nation of Islam rally in Detroit in 1962. The head of **Mosque** No. 7 in New York City, Malcolm was one of the top leaders in the Nation of Islam, and the two became fast friends. "Ali thought this was the smartest black man on the face of the earth because everything he said made sense," explained Ferdie Pacheco, Ali's doctor.

Malcolm X had joined the Nation of Islam in 1948 while in prison. After being released, he became known for his sharp mind and equally sharp tongue. He was a controversial figure who appeared on television, explaining the shocking views of the Nation of Islam. Ali was proud to have Malcolm X—who called the boxer his "little brother"—sitting ringside during his first fight with Sonny Liston.

Soon after, Malcolm X left the Nation of Islam due to arguments with Elijah Muhammad. Malcolm X had begun to change his mind about defining people just by their color and started a less controversial religious organization. Forced to pick a side, Ali stayed with the Nation of Islam. Malcolm X was assassinated in 1965, and years later Ali expressed great regret that he had rejected both his friend and his views at

The United States Postal Service honored Malcolm X's legacy by issuing this 33-cent stamp in 1999.

the time. "It was a pity and disgrace he died like that, because what Malcolm saw was right. . . . Color didn't make a man a devil. It's the heart, soul, and mind that counts."

punch"—a lightning-fast, right-handed chop to Liston's jaw that few in the audience could see. Liston may have not seen the punch, but he certainly felt it. He went sprawling onto his back. A shocked Ali stood over his opponent, shouting, "Get up and fight, sucker." Refusing the referee's orders to go to a corner of ring, Ali continued to taunt Liston, raising his arms in celebration of the knockdown. By the time Liston got up, it was too late. Ali had won. The crowd and much of the rest of the country may have not liked it, but Ali was still the Heavyweight champion of the world.

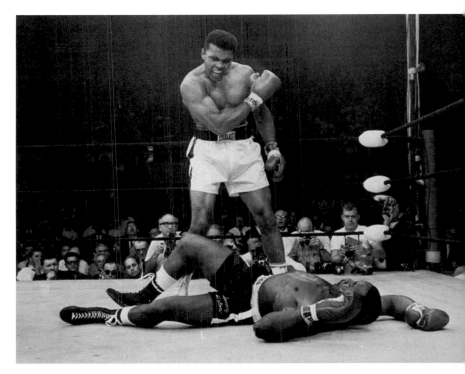

Ali's second fight with Sonny Liston did not even last one full round. Midway through the first round, Ali knocked out the challenger with a lightning-quick punch.

CHAPTER 6

Banished from Boxing

Man, I ain't got no quarrel with them Viet-cong.

While Muhammad Ali was training for his fights with Sonny Liston, America's war in Vietnam was raging thousands of miles away. At the time, the United States had a **draft** system that forced young men to join the military. For a while, Ali was one of those men who could be drafted. He was tested twice for military service in 1964; the athletic Ali aced the physical exams, but he failed the mental tests. "I said I was the greatest, not the smartest," explained the embarrassed boxer after the test results were revealed. Ali was reclassified from 1-A to 1-Y, meaning he was no longer qualified for service in the armed forces. That status, however, would change in time.

After defeating Liston the second time, the Heavyweight champion had little time to enjoy his victory. The press and public continued to attack him for his association with the Nation of Islam. His new religion wasn't working out so well at home, either. Ali's new wife tried to follow the Nation of Islam rules by going to lectures and eating the right foods. Proud of her good looks and fashion sense, Sonji refused to stop wearing makeup and refused to wear the long dresses that Muslim "sisters" wore. The young couple also argued about the religion's more questionable beliefs, and Ali soon had to pick between his wife and the Nation of Islam. He chose the latter, and separated from Sonji only months after they had married.

On November 22, 1965, Ali stepped into the ring to fight
another former Heavyweight champion, Floyd Patterson. As with
most of his fights, the buildup to the bout featured plenty of
promotion. Both boxers traded boasts, but things quickly became
personal. Speaking out for many, Patterson repeatedly insulted
Ali's Muslim beliefs: "I have nothing but contempt for the Black
Muslims and that for which they stand. . . . A Black Muslim as
the Heavyweight champion disgraces the sport and the nation."

From the opening bell, the older Patterson was clearly
outclassed. As the rounds wore on, Ali landed punches at will,
mixing in insults with his sharp jabs and painful body blows.
Ali could have knocked out Patterson whenever he wanted,
but instead he kept the former champion around for more
punishment. Finally, the referee stepped in to end the lopsided

Challenger Floyd Patterson struggles to get up after Ali knocked him down in the 12th
round of their championship fight in Las Vegas in 1965.

fight in the twelfth round. Ali won the fight, but an unhappy crowd booed him as he left the arena.

Even in winning, it seemed as if Ali was losing.

Choosing Not to Fight

By 1966, the need for more soldiers in Vietnam was growing. The military was forced to lower its test score requirements, and Ali was reclassified as 1-A on February 17, 1966. That meant he could be drafted at any moment. The press called Ali's home in Miami to find out his reaction. Question after question was tossed at Ali, who finally blurted out, "Man, I ain't got no quarrel with them **Viet-cong**." Without realizing it, Ali had just uttered one of his most famous statements—and one that hundreds of thousands of other young Americans were beginning to feel at the same time.

Ali was asking a serious

"Man, I ain't got no quarrel with them Viet-cong."

question: Why should he travel halfway around the world to fight against people he had never met—or that had never insulted him or his family or his friends—when he had battles to fight in his own country? The press, though, treated him like a traitor, afraid to fight for the United States.

Day after day, insulting newspaper articles were written, calling Ali a "sorry spectacle" who "squealed like a cornered rat" when asked to join the army. The general public's feelings against Ali only grew hotter. His next bout was supposed to be versus Ernie Terrell in Chicago, but protests against Ali caused it to be canceled. Ali instead fought a tough Canadian named George Chuvalo in Toronto on March 29, 1966. Even with the fight out of the country, calls to **boycott** Ali continued. A former boxing champion named Billy Conn was quoted as saying he'd "never

Ali arrives at a Veterans Administration office in 1966 to appeal the reclassification that made him eligible for the draft.

go to another one of his fights. [Ali] is a disgrace to the boxing profession. And I think that any American who pays to see him fight after what he has said recently should be ashamed."

Ali won the bout with a fifteen-round decision, pummeling Chuvalo round after round. However, Ali had become so controversial that many Americans refused to buy tickets for his fights or pay to watch them in theaters where they were shown live on large screens. Ali was as popular as ever overseas, however, so his next three fights were moved to Europe. First was a rematch with Henry Cooper in London in May. The English treated Ali like royalty, and a huge crowd of 45,000 watched the fighters brawl. Ali won in the sixth round after a dangerous cut above Cooper's left eye forced the referee to end

Vietnam

The Vietnam War was a complicated conflict involving more than a dozen countries. Hoping to stop the spread of **communism** within Asia, the United States began sending soldiers to Vietnam in the 1950s. The small conflict became an all-out war in the early 1960s, and soon after, thousands of young men were drafted and sent to fight in a country they knew almost nothing about. For years, the majority of Americans supported the war, believing it to be a worthy cause. However, with no clear end in sight and more and more young men being drafted, the antiwar movement was expanding at about the same time Ali refused to join the army. Failures in Vietnam, combined with ever-growing war protests, soured the country on the war. The United States eventually pulled out of Vietnam in 1973. Two years later, the war was officially over.

American soldiers are pictured in a bunker in Vietnam in 1968. The United States was involved in the fighting throughout the 1960s (and until 1973).

Ali joins the horses from the royal stables at Buckingham Palace for an early morning jog during his training for a fight against Henry Cooper in London in 1966.

the match. Three months later, Ali beat a fighter named Brian London, again in London. One month after that, he knocked out Karl Mildenberger in Frankfurt, Germany.

While Ali was fighting abroad, his lawyers in the United States were fighting to acquire an official conscientious-objector status for him. A conscientious objector is someone who refuses to fight in a country's army based on religious or moral grounds. Ali, who had been made a minister in the Nation of Islam, argued that his religion barred him from fighting in Vietnam. "How can I kill somebody when I pray five times a day for peace?" he asked.

As his case worked through the courts, Ali finally had a bout again back in the United States on November 14. In front of a huge crowd in Houston, Texas, Ali knocked out the hard-punching Cleveland Williams in the third round. At this point in his career, Ali was on an incredible roll, and even the boxing writers who couldn't stand Ali's religion and politics agreed that he had become one of the greatest Heavyweight fighters of all time.

Any goodwill Ali gained from that fight disappeared after his next bout against Ernie Terrell early in 1967. Even though Ali and Terrell had been friends in the past, the fight was a cruel one. Before the bout, Terrell refused to use the name Muhammad Ali, referring to the champ as Cassius Clay. Many members of the media had continued to do the same, and it seemed as if Ali decided to take all of his frustrations out on Terrell. Throughout the one-sided fight, Ali shouted "What's my name!" while throwing devastating combinations of punches. Terrell, who

Ali celebrates at the end of his 15-round fight with Ernie Terrell in 1967. Although he failed to knock out the challenger, Ali won by unanimous decision.

suffered a fracture under his left eye, gamely hung on for all fifteen rounds. As with his fight against Patterson just over a year earlier, Ali was seen as the villain even in victory.

On March 22, 1967, Ali stepped into the ring to fight Zora Folley in New York City. The champ knocked out Folley in the seventh round to bring his record to a phenomenal 29–0. Nobody knew it at the time, but it would be Ali's last professional fight for more than three years.

Banned from Boxing

After Ali's final attempt to be classified as a conscientious objector failed, he was ordered to report to the U.S. Armed Forces Examining and Entrance Station in Houston on April 28, 1967. On that day, twenty-six young men were ordered to join the army and be shipped to Fort Polk in Louisiana. Twenty-five of them agreed; but when asked to step forward to join the army, Ali silently refused. Even after being warned that refusing to join could mean five years in jail, Ali stood still.

Years later, Ali explained his decision: "I never thought of myself as great when I refused to go into the army. All I did was stand up for what I believed. There were people who thought the war in Vietnam was right. And those people, if they went to war, acted just as brave as I did."

Ali's enemies, though, cared little for his reasoning. Reaction to his refusal was swift. Only an hour later, the New York State Boxing Commission—without holding a trial or waiting to meet with Ali—suspended his boxing license. The other state commissions soon did the same, and the World Boxing Association took Ali's Heavyweight title away.

Soon after, Ali was put on trial for refusing induction into the army. He was quickly found guilty and sentenced to the

Several famous African American athletes joined Ali at this news conference in 1967 to support his decision not to fight in Vietnam. In the front row (left to right) are basketball's Bill Russell, Ali, football's Jim Brown, and basketball's Lew Alcindor (who would change his name to Kareem Abdul-Jabbar). In the back row (left to right) are politician Carl Stokes and football players Walter Beach, Bobby Mitchell, Sid Williams, Curtis McClinton, Willie Davis, Jim Shorter, and John Wooten.

maximum punishment: five years in jail and a $10,000 fine. Out on **bail** while his lawyers appealed the decision, Ali was free, but he wasn't allowed to leave the country. Barred from traveling abroad and banned from fighting in the United States, his life as a boxer was finished in the prime of his career, without his ever having lost in the ring.

Once again, newspapers were filled with stories attacking Ali for his outspoken views. At the same time, Ali also was gaining respect for standing by his beliefs in the face of incredible pressure. "He was, and is, one of my heroes," said Hall-of-Fame basketball star Kareem Abdul-Jabbar, who also changed his name (from Lew Alcindor) after converting to Islam as a young man. "To do what he did outside the ring, on top of being a brilliant one-of-a-kind athlete; that's a very hard hat to wear, and he wore it like he was born with it on."

In August of 1967, Ali married Belinda Boyd, a strict Muslim whom he had first met years earlier when she was a student at Chicago's University of Islam. Without his boxing income, Ali had to figure out ways to support his wife and growing family. His first child was a daughter named Maryum, born in 1968, and in 1970, Boyd gave birth to twin daughters, Jamillah and Rasheeda. Ali gave popular lectures at colleges across the country to make some money, talking about everything from Vietnam and segregation to his boxing career. With his legal fees growing by the day, he also took part in a documentary film about his life—called *A/K/A Cassius Clay*—and even starred in a Broadway musical called *Buck White*. To the surprise of many, reviews for Ali's singing and acting skills were good.

In his years spent away from boxing, some of Ali's more radical Nation of Islam views began to mellow as well. Whether it was on a college campus or out to eat in New York City, Ali was spending more time around people of all races and religions. While still a proud member of the Black Muslims, Ali no longer believed that whites were "blue-eyed

Ali's second marriage was to Belinda Boyd on August 17, 1967, in Chicago. Pictured here, the newlyweds enjoy a taste of their wedding cake.

devils" and the sole cause of society's problems. During this time, he still displayed flashes of his youthful anger and outrage, but he was also known to leave audiences roaring with laughter with his silly jokes and quick rhymes.

As this point in his life, Ali's boxing career had been taken away from him, and the government was working on throwing him in jail. Still, he never became bitter, handling himself instead with honor and dignity. He was showing more courage by sticking to a hugely unpopular decision than he ever showed in the ring. Without winning a boxing match, Ali slowly began winning over much of the public with his principled stand. Earlier in his career, he had said, "Some say I talk too much. But anything I say, I'm willing to back up." Nobody could doubt Ali's sincerity any longer.

Still, he never became bitter, handling himself instead with honor and dignity.

At the same time, the country's views on Vietnam were changing. In 1967, close to one hundred thousand people protested the war at a rally in Washington, D.C. The assassinations of civil rights activists Senator Robert Kennedy and Reverend Martin Luther King, Jr., in the following year made even more people realize that the country was on the wrong track. By 1970, public opinion of Ali and his refusal to fight in Vietnam had changed to the point at which he would soon be allowed to box again. However, with so much time lost, the question wasn't *should* he box—it was *could* he box after so much time off?

CHAPTER 7

The Fight of the Century

*This might shock and amaze ya
But I'm going to destroy Joe Frazier.*

For more than three years, the commissions that ruled boxing from state to state refused to let Muhammad Ali fight an official bout. It wasn't the government that banned Ali from making a living but rather this select group of powerful boxing figures, upset with Ali's outspoken views and refusal to join the army. The state of Georgia, however, didn't have a boxing commission. In the fall of 1970, the mayor of Atlanta, along with a state senator, decided that enough was enough. Ali deserved to fight again, so they helped organize a bout against a younger boxer named Jerry Quarry.

With the world watching, Ali returned to the ring on October 26, 1970. He looked a little older and a little thicker around the waist, but that didn't lessen the excitement one

After three years away from the ring, Ali returned to boxing against Jerry Quarry in 1970. He signs the agreement with Quarry (left) in this photo from September 10 of that year. The man between the two boxers is Leroy Johnson, a state senator from Georgia and boxing promoter who helped organize the fight.

bit. The crowd, filled with superstar athletes and actors along with Ali's mother and father, was almost entirely cheering for Ali. His three-and-a-half year exile from boxing had made him more popular than ever. Now even folks who didn't know the difference between a jab and an uppercut were rooting for Ali, who had become a symbol of courage.

Glad to be back in the spotlight, Ali was in high spirits. Minutes before the fight, he popped his head into the dressing room of the younger Quarry. "You best be in good shape," he said with a smile, "because if you whup me, you've whupped the greatest fighter in the whole wide world."

Early in the fight, Ali connected with several strong combinations of punches, one of which opened a cut above Quarry's left eye. The cut left Quarry unable to continue, and Ali won by a TKO in the third round. Soon after the fight, Ali's lawyers argued that Ali was being discriminated against for his religious beliefs by not being allowed to box in New York State. They won the case, and Ali was once again legally allowed to box across the country. Six weeks after fighting Quarry, Ali fought and beat another boxer, this time knocking out his opponent in Round 15. He still looked rusty and a step slower than he had been before his long break from boxing, but Ali was back and ready to fight for what he believed was rightfully his—the Heavyweight championship of the world.

A Battle for the Ages

The sport of boxing, of course, had kept on going during Ali's absence. After Ali was stripped of his title, tournaments and additional fights were held to determine the new Heavyweight champion. By 1970, "Smokin'" Joe Frazier, an aggressive brawler out of Philadelphia, Pennsylvania, had become the undisputed

"Smokin'" Joe Frazier

One of the toughest Heavyweight boxers in history, Joe Frazier was born on a humble farm in South Carolina on January 12, 1944. The second-youngest child in a family of thirteen, Frazier loved watching boxing matches as a kid, and he decided early on that he wanted to be a fighter. With no money to train in a gym, Frazier built his own punching bags, stuffing them with anything he could get his hands on—old clothes, boots, and even corn cobs.

At the age of fifteen, Frazier headed north to leave the Jim Crow laws of the South behind. In Philadelphia, his ring skills rapidly improved; after winning three Golden Gloves, Frazier won a gold medal at the 1964 Olympics in Tokyo, Japan. He turned pro the following year, and quickly became known for his bruising style and powerful left hook.

Frazier knocked out many of the finest Heavyweights in his generation, but he's best known for his three bouts with Muhammad Ali. Between 1971 and 1975, the two proud boxers fought a total of forty-one incredible rounds. "I don't think two big men ever fought fights like me and Joe Frazier," Ali has said. "Of all the men I fought in boxing, Sonny Liston was the scariest, George Foreman was the most powerful, Floyd Patterson was the most skilled as a boxer. But the roughest and toughest was Joe Frazier."

In Ali's absence from the ring, Joe Frazier, shown here in 1970, became the Heavyweight champion. Ali and Frazier agreed to fight for the first time in New York City in 1971.

Heavyweight champion. Unbeaten and unafraid, Frazier jumped at the chance to fight Ali. He knew he'd never be fully respected as the champion until he beat Ali.

Their bout, which was scheduled for New York City's famed Madison Square Garden on March 8, 1971, was promoted as the Fight of the Century. For the first time in history, two undefeated Heavyweight boxers, both with a genuine claim to the championship title, would battle in the ring. Each boxer was paid $2,500,000—a record amount at that time—and the hype was greater than anything that had come before it.

Ali took his famed prefight routine to a new level. "There's not a man alive who can whup me. I'm too fast. I'm too smart.

The Poet Pugilist

At a press conference a few days before the Fight of the Century, Ali proved that his break from boxing hadn't damaged his poetic skills. He recited another of his celebrated rhymes.

Joe's gonna come out smokin'
But I ain't gonna be jokin'
I'll be pickin' and pokin'
Pouring water on his smokin'
This might shock and amaze ya
But I'm going to destroy Joe Frazier.

Always a showman, Ali entertained media and the fans by making up poems before many of his matches. This photo of the confident Ali was taken just two days before his bout against Joe Frazier.

I'm too pretty," he said to a crowd of writers. "I should be a postage stamp. That's the only way I'll ever get licked."

Such talk was expected, but Ali's war of words also took on a sharper tone. Frazier started off with plenty of respect for Ali. That esteem dated to the time Ali encouraged Frazier to go pro after his 1964 Olympic gold medal. In fact, Frazier had even offered to lend Ali money during his time away from the ring. However, Frazier quickly lost all respect after Ali repeatedly called him ugly and dumb. Not nearly as quick with words as Ali, Frazier struggled to answer back. Even worse, Ali began saying that Frazier—who had a much tougher upbringing in the South than Ali did—didn't stand up for the black man. Ali set himself up as the true black champion, while calling Frazier a pretender who didn't deserve the support of black people. Thirty years after the fight, Frazier was still furious. "Anything that came to his mind about me, he said. And he meant every word that he said. It did not just hurt then. It still hurts."

Frazier knew boxing matches weren't decided by who could say the funniest thing or had the most supporters. He couldn't wait to get into the ring to earn the respect he so desperately desired.

The Battle Begins

As the challenger, Ali danced into the ring for the Fight of the Century first, following trainer Angelo Dundee and the rest of his crew in matching bright red-and-white outfits. Frazier entered next in a stylish green-and-yellow robe with "World Champion" stitched on the back. After receiving instructions from the referee, the boxers retreated to their corners and waited for the opening bell. The time for talking was over. More than 20,000 fans cheered, while millions more in dozens of countries settled into their seats to watch the fight on closed-circuit television. One of the most publicized boxing matches ever was about to become one of the most famous as well.

The opening rounds were evenly matched. The boxers bobbed and weaved around the ring, trading powerful blows. As usual, Ali talked to his opponent and played to the crowd, shaking his head when Frazier connected with a punch and bragging to the ringside press. Frazier kept moving forward, ignoring Ali's taunts, responding not with words but with more punches. Every jab and hook that connected sent a jolt of electricity through the crowd, bringing the fans to their feet.

Ali won a few of the early rounds, but Frazier's nonstop assault was beginning to take its toll by the middle of the fight. Resting on his feet instead of bouncing on his toes, Ali was no longer dancing in the ring. Instead he tried to out-punch the stronger Frazier. Too often, he laid back against the ropes, taking punch after punch to his arms and body. In Round 11, Frazier wobbled Ali with a powerful left hook. A couple of rounds later,

This photograph shows a rare sight: Ali sprawled on the canvas. Joe Frazier (in the green trunks) has just connected on a vicious left hook that knocked Ali down. But the boxer managed to get up and continue the fight.

Ali managed to reenergize long enough to stun Frazier, sending the crowd into a frenzy.

The fifteenth, and final, round started with both boxers exhausted. In the words of one ringside writer, the two boxers were "draped over each other, looking like big fish who had wallowed onto a beach." Somehow, Frazier found the strength to deliver one final mighty blow—a left hook that landed square on Ali's jaw, sending him straight down onto the canvas. A dazed Ali popped up immediately, valiantly fighting back until the round and fight ended. "The way they were hitting, I was surprised that it went fifteen [rounds]. They threw some of the best punches I've ever seen," said the man with the best view in the arena, referee Arthur Mercante.

The winner, and still Heavyweight champion of the world is determined to be Joe Frazier, by unanimous decision.

Their faces bruised, the two warriors staggered to their corners after the final bell. Within minutes, the judges' scorecards were tallied. Frazier was declared the winner by unanimous decision. Ali had been handed his first loss as a professional boxer.

"Let's get out of here. Let's go home." a dejected Ali said to his crew. Before he could leave the ring, Frazier—in as much pain as Ali, if not more—approached Ali.

"You're a real tough man," Frazier said.

"You are, too," answered Ali. "You're the champ."

CHAPTER 8

Warrior Spirit

I lost it. But I didn't shed one tear. I got to keep living. I'm not ashamed.

After Muhammad Ali lost his first professional fight to Joe Frazier, his enemies celebrated loudly. To many, Ali had finally received the beating that he deserved. The Louisville Lip had finally been beaten, and it was time to rejoice. Red Smith, a famous sportswriter at the time, wrote a column on the hard-fought battle, claiming that if Ali and Frazier fought a dozen times, Frazier would win all twelve bouts—and each fight would only get easier for him. Even some people in Ali's own corner were beginning to whisper that the champ had lost a step and that his glory days were probably behind him.

One person who never lost faith, however, was Ali himself. The years he had spent banned from boxing had given him a strong taste of hardship. He'd already lost millions of dollars in potential earnings, been pulled to pieces by the press, and had been booed by thousands of his countrymen. One loss wasn't going to shake his faith in himself or his beliefs.

Shortly after the fight, Ali agreed to be interviewed by a pair of high school students for their school newspaper. After being asked what it felt like to lose, Ali took a deep breath and answered: "Oh, they all said that if he ever loses, he'll shoot himself, he'll die; but I'm human. I've lost

The day after losing his first professional fight, Ali got behind the wheel of his van and headed out of New York City. He'd be back in the ring in less than five months.

one fight out of thirty-two, and it was a decision that could have gone another way . . . I lost it But I didn't shed one tear. I got to keep living. I'm not ashamed."

Around the same time, Ali had an unexpected ally on his quest to keep on living with his head held high—the U.S. Supreme Court. On June 28, 1971, the Court reversed Ali's conviction for refusing induction into the U.S. Army. Ali could now sleep soundly at night as he knew for certain he wouldn't be going to jail for holding to his beliefs.

The Long March Back

The Supreme Court's decision also meant Ali was free again to travel wherever and whenever he wanted. An excited Ali knew that millions of fans around the globe would line up to see him train and fight. First, though, he had a scheduled fight against an old friend named Jimmy Ellis. Ali and Ellis had grown up near one another in Louisville, and for years Ellis had worked with Ali as a sparring partner. Because Ellis had sparred with Ali for thousands of rounds in practice, he figured he could beat his former boss. He guessed wrong—on July 26, Ali knocked out Ellis in Round 12 with a sharp right-hand punch.

Ali and his **entourage** packed their bags and began to tour the world. Everywhere he went, crowds followed, and Ali soaked up the attention like a giant sponge. From signing autographs at press conferences to giving street-corner magic shows to crowds of laughing children, Ali enjoyed his reputation as the "people's champion."

Ali hadn't given up on his quest to regain the real Heavyweight championship, either. Over the next year and a half, he had an impressive string of nine straight wins against a mix of boxers, ranging from former champion Floyd Patterson to lesser fighters such as Al Lewis and Joe Bugner. Along with bouts in New York, Nevada, and Texas, he took on challengers in Canada, Switzerland, Ireland, and Japan. Throughout all of this traveling, Ali found time to go on his first pilgrimage (journey to a sacred place) to Mecca, an important ritual for Muslims. He

Jimmy Ellis was a friend of Ali's from Louisville. But that didn't stop Ali from driving repeated blows to his face, as depicted in this photograph from the July 26 match, until he ended their fight with a 12th-round knockout.

also fathered his first son, named Muhammad Eban, with his wife Belinda.

Ali's popularity was at an all-time high. In the summer of 1972, Hollywood even came knocking at Ali's door, offering him the starring role—and a hefty paycheck—in a remake of a movie called *Here Comes Mr. Jordan*. Elijah Muhammad, leader of the Nation of Islam, disliked the movie's plot and asked Ali not to take part. A frustrated Ali agreed and turned his attention instead to another lifelong dream, building a new training camp called Deer Lake in rural Pennsylvania.

Deer Lake

In the fall of 1972, Ali purchased several wooded acres in the Blue Mountains west of Allentown, Pennsylvania. Ever since he had worked out at Archie Moore's Salt Mine training camp in 1960, Ali dreamed of having a camp of his own. Naming it Deer Lake, Ali built a boxing gym in the center of the property and placed a series of log cabins and a mess hall around it. Eventually, the compound would grow to eighteen stand-alone buildings, including a tiny mosque painted bright white.

Lifting an idea from Moore's camp, Ali trucked in boulders and had his father paint the names of boxing greats past and present on them—from Sugar Ray Robinson and Joe Louis to Sonny Liston and George Foreman. Scores of well-known visitors, such as singers Elvis Presley and Frank Sinatra, would sit by these rocks or around the camp's giant fire pit, listening to Ali brag and boast. However, one didn't have to be famous to visit: Deer Lake was open to anyone who cared to stop by. Ali was happy to spend time telling stories, and his favorite visitors were kids. The champ would often take an entire afternoon off from training to laugh and show off his many magic tricks.

Ali fulfilled a dream when he built his own large training center called Deer Lake in Pennsylvania. Here, Ali looks on as heavyweight Floyd Patterson works out at the new center in 1972.

With Ali working on his winning streak, everything seemed to be pointing toward a storybook rematch with Joe Frazier for the championship belt.

However, in early 1973, two obstacles got in the way. In January, Frazier stepped into the ring against an up-and-coming boxer named George Foreman. The hard-punching Foreman, who had been knocking down

. . . everything seemed to be pointing toward a storybook rematch with Joe Frazier for the championship belt.

Heavyweights as easily as a mower cuts through grass, sent Frazier to the mat six times in just two rounds, winning the championship belt with stunning ease.

Then in late March, Ali fought a former marine named Ken Norton. Previously a sparring partner of Frazier's, Norton wasn't considered much of a threat. His awkward fighting style, however, confused the overconfident Ali from the start. And in the second round, Norton connected with a sharp punch that broke Ali's jaw. Ali bravely battled on, refusing to stop the fight, but the injury, combined with Norton's rising confidence, proved to be too great. While Ali gained the respect of boxing fans for fighting through terrible pain, Norton won the fight by a unanimous decision. Ali dropped another notch in ranking—he was one step further from regaining the championship title.

True Grit

To fix Ali's broken jaw, doctors had to wire his mouth shut after the fight. Even that didn't stop Ali from talking, and two weeks later he outlined his plans at a press conference. He would win rematches against Norton and Frazier, and then take on the current champion Foreman to win back the title.

Ali lands a vicious right hook during his rematch with Ken Norton in 1973.

It took six months for the jaw to fully heal, but true to his word, Ali trained furiously at Deer Lake, chopping wood and taking long runs, for his march back to the top ranking. "I took a nobody and created a monster," Ali said before his rematch with Norton. "Now I have to punish him bad." Once again, Norton proved to be a tough match, but this time Ali prevailed, winning the twelve-round fight by a unanimous decision.

The stage had been set for Ali's long-awaited rematch with Frazier. After a final warm-up fight in Indonesia against Rudi

Lubbers, Ali signed to fight Frazier on January 28, 1974. Once again, the fight was to be held in New York City's Madison Square Garden. Again, the two boxers' prefight chatter quickly became personal. Frazier made no secret of hating Ali. "There's something wrong with this guy," he claimed. "I'm aware now that the guy's got a couple of loose screws someplace." Ali returned the favor by continuing to call Frazier uneducated.

Less than a week before the fight, the two fighters were taping a television talk show together. A heated argument quickly started, and Ali called Frazier ignorant. The insult was one too

Tempers are starting to flare between Ali and Joe Frazier during the taping of a television show in 1974. A scuffle soon broke out, and the fighters had to be separated. Several days later, the two battled in the ring.

many for Frazier, who leapt up to challenge Ali. Thinking it was all part of the prefight publicity, Ali playfully stepped forward and grabbed Frazier. Frazier, though, was looking for a real fight, and he threw Ali down to the floor. Before any punches could be thrown, the fighters were separated. The two men were fined $5,000 by the New York State Boxing Commission for nearly starting a brawl.

The match now had all the buzz it needed, and the air in the sold-out arena was electric when it finally started. Ali was in far better shape than he had been in their previous battle, and he had a better strategy as well. Instead of boxing in close with Frazier, Ali now used his quick jab to keep Frazier away. Ali came close to knocking Frazier out in the second round, and except for a few rounds in the middle of the fight, Ali controlled the tempo and landed more punches. After the twelfth round ended, Ali was announced the winner by a unanimous decision.

A bruised but furious Frazier demanded another rematch. Ali agreed. "I'm not gonna duck Joe. I'm gonna give Joe all the chances he wants." That would come later. First, though, Ali had earned his shot at reclaiming the championship by fighting the undefeated George Foreman.

After the twelfth round ended, Ali was announced the winner by a unanimous decision.

CHAPTER 9

The Rumble in the Jungle

I'm so mean I make medicine sick.

After beating Joe Frazier in their second match, Muhammad Ali was ready once again to claim the title of Heavyweight champion of the world. There was a rather large problem in the way, however, and that problem's name was George Foreman. In the world of boxing, there is nothing more intimidating than a talented Heavyweight with a dominant knockout punch. No matter how well one boxes against such a fighter, all it takes is one solid punch to lose the fight. And when George Foreman knocked somebody down, more often than not that fighter didn't get back up.

How good was the twenty-six-year-old Foreman? Before his fight with Ali, Foreman boasted a perfect 40–0 record, thirty-seven of which he had won by knockout. In fact, Foreman had won his last twenty-four fights by knockout, including easy second-round wins over Frazier and Norton—both of whom had beaten Ali.

Ali came into the fight with a still-impressive 44–2 lifetime record, but everyone knew that the thirty-two-year-old boxer was no longer at the top of his game. His last several fights proved that Ali had a strong chin—meaning he could take a bruising and keep on fighting—but his speed had decreased dramatically. Ali could no longer rely on lightning-fast reflexes and fancy footwork. Instead, he had to out-think his opponents.

Before the Rumble in the Jungle in 1974, Ali (right) and George Foreman (left) are praised by Mobutu Sese Seko, the leader of Zaire.

Mismatch or not, every fight fan was excited about these two giants of the sport squaring off. After many locations were considered, Kinshasa, Zaire, was chosen as the site for the fight. Zaire's president/dictator Mobutu Sese Seko offered a staggering $10 million dollars to host the fight, believing the bout would help spread both his name and the name of his country around the world. Now that the fight was to be held in Africa—a continent known for animal safaris and sweeping wilderness— it got its famous nickname: the Rumble in the Jungle.

Ali, Bomma-Ya!

The Rumble between Ali and Foreman was originally scheduled to take place on September 25, 1974. Ali showed up several weeks early, bringing along a crew of more than thirty

George Foreman

Today, George Foreman is a lovable celebrity, famous for his winning smile and for selling a popular countertop grilling machine. But when he was younger, Foreman was one of the most feared men in boxing. Born desperately poor on January 10, 1949, Foreman had a rough childhood in a Houston **ghetto**. A street fighter and bully, Foreman was frequently in trouble with the law. Hoping to make a better life for himself, Foreman joined the Job Corps—a government agency dedicated to ending poverty—and it was there that he began training as a boxer.

At nineteen, Foreman won the gold medal at the 1968 Olympics in Mexico City. By 1973, the hard-punching Foreman had become the Heavyweight champion by hitting Joe Frazier with an uppercut that literally lifted Frazier off his feet. A few years after his Rumble in the Jungle against Ali, Foreman retired from boxing to become a Christian minister. A decade later, a far heavier Foreman returned to the ring at the age of thirty-eight. Most boxing fans figured it was a stunt to make some easy money, but Foreman shocked the boxing world by eventually winning the Heavyweight championship. He was forty-five-years-old at the time.

Once one of the most feared boxers in the world, George Foreman is now famous as a mild-mannered television pitchman and reality star, as seen in this 2008 photograph.

people. Some of those in his group, such as trainer Angelo Dundee and Ali's cook Lana Shabazz, had important jobs to do. Most were there just because Ali liked having them around.

Ali stayed within Mobutu's presidential compound, a vast spread forty miles from the city of Kinshasa that included an Olympic-sized pool and a small zoo. He trained hard, but he also left frequently to interact with the people of Zaire, touring their villages and stopping to play with children. Though homesick in private, Ali was impressed by what he saw in Zaire, and he let his feelings be known. Here was a country run by black people. The soldiers were black, the doctors were black, and even the

The fans in Zaire loved Ali. In this photograph, many of them cheer as he drives past on a sightseeing tour.

airline pilots were black—a fact that seemed to calm the flight-phobic Ali.

In return, the locals treated Ali like a hero. Fans swarmed him wherever he left the compound, cheering him on as if he, and not Foreman, were the champion. As Ali jogged along the roads to adjust to fighting in the country's hot climate, crowds around him would chant "Ali, bomma-ya"—meaning "Ali, kill him." Ali would chant it back, smiling the whole time.

Foreman, on the other hand, wore a scowl for nearly his entire stay in Zaire. It was obvious that he'd rather be back home in America and the only thing that seemed to make him happy was his pet German shepherd, Daggo, that he had brought to Africa. At press conferences, Foreman kept his answers short and direct. When a reporter asked if he, like Ali, liked to talk much in the ring, his answer was simple. "I never get a chance to talk much in the ring. By the time I begin to know a fellow, it's over."

Doing what he did best, Ali entertained the international press with a new collection of poems and boasts. He took to calling Foreman "the Mummy," claiming "he moves like a slow mummy, and there ain't no mummy gonna whup the great Muhammad Ali." He later bragged that Foreman would have so many nicks and cuts on his face after the fight it would look like he had "a bad morning shave."

"I never get a chance to talk much in the ring. By the time I begin to know a fellow, it's over."

Eight days before the fight was to take place, Foreman did get a nasty cut just below his eyebrow while sparring. The match had to be postponed for several weeks to let the injury heal. A brooding Foreman hunkered down even deeper, while

Sting Like a Bee

Before the fight, most believed Foreman would knock Ali senseless. If Ali was scared, he never let it show. Instead, he continued his tradition of putting down his opponents in rhyme. The following poem left writers at a press conference howling with laughter:

> Float like a butterfly, sting like a bee
> His hands can't hit what his eyes can't see
> Now you see me, now you don't
> George thinks he will, but I know he won't
> I done wrassled with an alligator
> I done tussled with a whale
> Only last week I murdered a rock
> Injured a stone, hospitalized a brick
> I'm so mean I make medicine sick.

Ali continued to laugh and train, followed wherever he went by cheers of "Ali, bomma-ya."

The Rumble

The Rumble in the Jungle took place on October 30, 1974. The fight started at 4:00 a.m. so it would be on television in the early evening in the United States. Close to 60,000 fans crammed into Kinshasa's stadium, and a giant portrait of Mobutu, the country's ruler, towered above the crowd.

Ali may have been bragging for weeks about how he was going to take down the Mummy, but his dressing room before the fight was strangely quiet. Friends feared for his safety—Foreman was that dangerous. Before leaving for the ring, Ali faced his friends. "This ain't nothing but another day in the dramatic life of Muhammad Ali. Do I look scared?" he asked. "I fear Allah and thunderstorms and bad plane rides, but this is like another day in the gym." At the same time, the people in Foreman's dressing room were so confident they were praying for *Ali's* safety, worried that Foreman might seriously injure Ali with one of his punches.

From the moment the fight began, Ali proved to the world that he truly wasn't scared. At the opening bell, he rushed straight forward and landed a punch on Foreman's head. Then, surprising even his own corner, Ali refused to dance and hide from the powerful champion. Instead, when cornered, Ali simply leaned back against the ropes, letting Foreman swing away. Ali's corner pleaded with him to dance away from Foreman, but he refused.

. . . Ali simply leaned back against the ropes, letting Foreman swing away.

"I won't kid you. When he went to the ropes, I felt sick,' Ali's trainer Dundee admitted later. What Dundee, Foreman, and everyone else didn't realize yet was that Ali had a plan. Over the next couple of rounds, he continued to lean against the ropes, letting Foreman swing away. Because of the way Ali covered himself, most of Foreman's punches landed on his arms and gloves, not on his body or head. The champion connected on some of his blows, but most missed their target and his energy was slowly draining away with each punch thrown. Later on, Ali's decision to tire out Foreman became known as the rope-a-dope strategy, but at the time, most of the crowd thought Ali had lost his mind.

This is the famous rope-a-dope strategy that spurred Ali to victory over George Foreman in Zaire in 1974. Foreman's blows are not damaging to Ali, who has covered himself against the ropes. Instead, all of those punches only served to tire out Foreman.

In the middle of Round 3, Ali began firing back, staggering Foreman with a combination of punches. In the following round, Ali started challenging the champion. "Is that the best you can do?" he dared. "That's a sissy punch." Howling with excitement, the crowd chanted "Ali, bomma-ya, Ali, bomma-ya" between rounds. The impossible, it seemed, was happening.

By the eighth round, an exhausted Foreman stood up from his stool slowly. Ali's nickname for him, the Mummy, was coming true. As Foreman threw his heavy, but still dangerous, punches in slow motion, Ali gave up his rope-a-dope strategy and began firing back with stinging combinations. Like a towering redwood tree being attacked by a crew of lumberjacks, Ali's blows finally caused the giant Foreman to come crashing down with only ten seconds left in the round. As the referee counted Foreman out, Ali raised his arms and was swarmed by his friends.

Once again, against the odds, Ali was the Heavyweight champion of the world.

"Fair and Square"

After being beaten in Zaire, Foreman was full of excuses—the count was too fast, the fight delay ruined his training. Nevertheless, years later, he spoke proudly about his role in one of the greatest fights in boxing history: "I realized I'd lost to a great champion; probably the greatest of all time. . . . He won fair and square, and now I'm just proud to be part of the Ali legend. If people mention my name with his from time to time, that's enough for me. That, and I hope Muhammad likes me, because I like him. I like him a lot."

CHAPTER 10

The World's Champion

[Ali almost] never declined when asked for an autograph, handshake, or kiss. As far as he was concerned, people were people, and all people were meant to be loved.

—Jim Brown

Muhammad Ali's surprise victory over George Foreman rocketed his fame to even greater heights. After the Rumble in the Jungle, he had become the most famous athlete—and perhaps even the most famous person—in the world. For many people, be it an athlete or a movie star, such fame soon becomes overwhelming, forcing a

Ali returned from his surprise victory over George Foreman to the cheers of fans at Chicago's Midway Airport.

retreat to a more private life out of the public's gaze. Ali's pride and happiness, though, only grew under the heat of the spotlight.

The Heavyweight champion returned home from Africa to a hero's welcome. At the end of 1974, *Ring* magazine honored Ali with their Fighter of the Year award. In addition, Ali, wearing a fancy tuxedo and a wide grin, graced the cover of *Sports Illustrated* as their prestigious Sportsman of the Year.

At the same time, Ali was also invited to his first of many visits to the White House by President Gerald Ford. A former athlete,

. . . Ali, wearing a fancy tuxedo and a wide grin, graced the cover of Sports Illustrated *. . .*

Ford looked forward to shaking hands with the champ. However, the president also admitted he had invited Ali to help heal the wounds caused by the Vietnam War. President Ford understood that Ali had become an ambassador for millions of people in the United States and around the world. Only a few years after the government had tried to throw Ali into jail, he was in the White House, joking with the president. "You made a big mistake in letting me come," Ali told Ford, "because now I'm going after your job."

You didn't have to be the president to gain Ali's attention. The world Heavyweight champion continued to host a steady stream of visitors at his Deer Lake training camp. He also visited schools, hospitals, and just about any other place he was invited. He'd happily stop and chat with strangers, kissing babies as if he really was running for president. "Most celebrities live life removed from their [fans]," Jim Brown, a Hall-of-Fame football star and friend of Ali's, once explained. "Ali chose to walk among

'Wherever he went in the world, Ali was surrounded by people—many of them adoring youngsters.

them, never looking down at those who looked up to him. He loved to be recognized, and virtually never declined when asked for an autograph, handshake, or kiss. As far was he was concerned, people were people, and all people were meant to be loved."

Rolling with the Punches

On February 25, 1975, Elijah Muhammad, the Nation of Islam's leader, passed away. At that time, Ali's relationship with the Nation of Islam had been through some rocky years. The Nation's strict rules banned not only such things as alcohol, unhealthy foods, and gambling, but also sports. Originally willing to overlook Ali's boxing career, the group's leader eventually banned Ali temporarily from being an official minister and from giving lectures in the group's mosques. Ali still considered Elijah Muhammad a great man, however, and had even purchased a mansion near the leader's home in Chicago to be closer to him.

Ali was at his Deer Lake training camp when he heard the news that Muhammad had passed and that Elijah's son Wallace was taking over. Wallace immediately toned down many of the religion's more controversial beliefs, particularly those that had to do with race. For the champion, who had faithfully stuck by

Ali addresses a Nation of Islam meeting in 1975. To the immediate left, seated, is Wallace Muhammad, the son of Elijah Muhammad, who is pictured behind. Wallace took over as the leader of the Nation of Islam after his father's death.

others of a different race, such as his trainer Angelo Dundee and doctor Ferdie Pacheco, the changes were cause for celebration. Wallace's new tone would eventually cause a major split within the Nation of Islam, but Ali was elated that anyone could now join his religion if he or she felt a calling. "Wallace is showing us there are good and bad regardless of color, that the devil is in the mind and heart, not the skin. We Muslims hate injustice and evil, but we don't have time to hate people," Ali said at the time.

Ali's outlook on his boxing life continued to be undeniably positive as well. At one point, he claimed his next match was going to be against both Frazier and Foreman, and that he'd fight them back-to-back on the same night. That fight never happened, but in March, Ali did square off against a **journeyman** named Chuck Wepner. Even though the fight was an easy one for Ali, it still took him fifteen rounds to knock out Wepner, whose nose was broken early in the bout.

Except for two bouts against far inferior opponents, all of Ali's remaining fights would take at least ten rounds. In May, Ali defeated Ron Lyle with a knockout in Round 11, and in June, he won a fifteen-round decision against Joe Bugner. Ali was winning, but in doing so, he was being hit with a huge number of punches. Some experts, both in and out of Ali's camp, were beginning to wonder if he should retire, leaving the sport while still a champion and in good health. Instead, Ali had a promise he wanted to keep: Joe Frazier had demanded a rematch after their last fight, and a rematch he was going to get.

The Thrilla in Manila

Ali had his third and final fight with Frazier just outside of Manila, the capital of the Philippines. The fight's promoters

Philippines President Ferdinand Marcos applauds as Ali makes a playful face at Joe Frazier two weeks before their title fight in Manila. Imelda Marcos, Ferdinand's wife, stands between the two boxers.

quickly dubbed the match the Thrilla in Manila, and just as in the boxers' previous two battles, everyone who watched received more than their money's worth.

The fight was scheduled for October 1, 1975, and Ali once again brought along a huge following. His contract for the fight, which earned the champ more than $6 million, requested rooms for fifty people in total. When he arrived in Manila, he even told the hotel he needed two more rooms. One of the members of Ali's entourage was a former model that he'd been having an affair with for the past year. Her presence in Manila became one of the bigger stories before the match.

Despite the strict rules of his Muslim faith, Ali was not a faithful husband. When he flew to Manila, he asked his wife Belinda to stay behind instead of traveling with him as she typically did. At that time, Ali had six children—four with Belinda and two from other relationships outside of marriage—and Belinda stayed home to take care of the kids. However, Ali had another reason for wanting his wife to say home—her name was Veronica Porche. Ali originally met Porche before the Rumble in the Jungle, and it was a poorly kept secret that the two of them had formed a relationship.

Before the fight, Ali met with the president of the Philippines, Ferdinand Marcos, who mistakenly called Porche Ali's wife. When

Ali met Veronica Porche before the Rumble in the Jungle against George Foreman. Eventually, Ali and Veronica were married. The couple is seen here, enjoying a night at the Cotton Club, a famous nightclub in New York City.

news of this made an important magazine in the United States, a furious and insulted Belinda flew straight to Manila to confront her husband. After a heated argument, she stormed out of Ali's hotel straight back to the plane she came in on for a return flight home.

Ali's wife wasn't the only person unhappy with the champ. That Ali and Frazier were not friends was already old news. However, the buildup to the fight showed that, if anything, the time off between their last fight and the one to come had made them dislike each other even more. With other boxers, Ali's taunting routine usually had a comical edge, and he knew not to take cutting remarks too far. With Frazier, Ali seemed not to know when to stop. Again Ali referred to Frazier as ignorant, and he soon took to calling Frazier a gorilla. "It will be a killer . . . and a thrilla, when I get the gorilla in Manila," he rhymed. Ali began carrying around a tiny toy gorilla, punching it and telling the press it was Frazier.

Even a champion debater would have trouble taking on Ali in a press conference, and a man of few words like Frazier had no chance winning such a war. Ali's words fueled his anger, and Frazier knew that his only chance to get revenge would be in the ring. "It's real hatred," Frazier told the press before the fight. "I want to hurt him. I don't want to knock him out. I want to take his heart out."

A "Thrilla" to the End

When the Thrilla in Manila started, it appeared that Frazier wouldn't be getting the revenge he so desperately desired. Ali controlled the early rounds, outboxing the challenger, steadily landing his jabs, and buckling Frazier's legs several times.

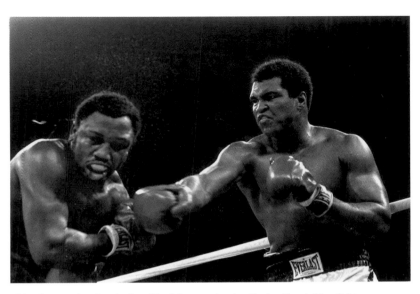

Ali lands a punch in his third, and final, bout against Joe Frazier. The thrilling fight ended with both boxers exhausted after 14 grueling rounds.

The two boxers, though, had been through far too much together for the fight to end early or be one-sided. In the fourth round, Frazier's relentless assault began to wear Ali down, and his booming punches began hitting their target. "Old Joe Frazier, why I thought you were washed up," Ali said to the challenger as the seventh round began. "Somebody told you all wrong, pretty boy," Frazier answered, crashing another powerful punch into Ali.

In the following rounds, the two fighters threw away technique and simply brawled, exchanging punch after powerful punch. Fueled by pride and determination, both fighters rose to their best. In Round 13, Ali landed a hook so powerful it sent Frazier's mouthpiece flying into the crowd. Ali continued his assault in Round 14, battering Frazier's left eye shut. Ali had taken just as much damage, however, and both boxers staggered back to their corners when the round ended.

Exhausted, Ali ordered his corner to cut off his gloves—he couldn't fight any longer. Dundee ignored Ali's pleas, telling the champ he had only one more round to fight. Meanwhile, across the ring, Eddie Futch, Frazier's trainer, surveyed the damage to his fighter. "Sit down, son," he said. "It's all over. No one will ever forget what you did here today." Futch couldn't let Frazier take any more damage. He ended the fight. Ali was the winner.

It was a lucky break for Ali, who was as tired as he'd ever been in the ring. "Frazier quit just before I did," he said. "I didn't think I could fight anymore." Ali remained the Heavyweight champion of the world, but Frazier was far from the loser. Both boxers, their faces badly battered, proved to the world that they each had the courage and heart of a true champion.

Futch couldn't let Frazier take any more damage. He ended the fight.

Soon after the fight ended, a reporter inside the ring asked Ali about Frazier. "He's the greatest fighter of all time," an exhausted Ali whispered. "Next to me."

CHAPTER 11

Throwing in the Towel

For the first time, I feel like I'm forty years old. I know it's the end; I'm not crazy.

Muhammad Ali had no way of knowing it at the time, but the Thrilla in Manila was to be his last great boxing match. Nowadays, it's clear Ali should have retired after beating Joe Frazier. He had nothing more to prove. His popularity was at an all-time high. He was still in relatively good health. By retiring, Ali could have left boxing while he was still at the top of his game, as a champion.

For many athletes, the toughest decision they ever have to make is picking the right time to leave the sport they love. As athletes grow older, their knowledge of their sport only grows. Mentally, they're as tough as they've ever been. However, their bodies don't respond as fast as they

Even though Ali beat Joe Frazier in their third fight, he knew the end of his boxing career was near. He's pictured here in 1978 in his home in Chicago.

once did. They are injured more quickly, and recovery takes longer. Quitting, though, means saying good-bye to the thrill of competition and the cheering crowds. It means saying good-bye to the large paychecks. It also means saying good-bye to doing the thing they do best.

By the end of 1975, boxing had been the focus of Ali's life for more than twenty years. The sport was not something he could easily give up. Ali talked of possibly retiring after his third fight with Frasier, but instead of hanging up his boxing gloves he decided to return to the ring—for better and for worse.

Easy Does It

Ali fought three matches in the first half of 1976, each against clearly outmatched opponents. The first was against Jean-Pierre Coopman, Belgium's Heavyweight champion. Though nicknamed the Lion of Flanders, Coopman was little more than a pussycat compared to Ali. The champion laughed and joked with television crews during the fight, and he stretched it into the fifth round before knocking Coopman out.

Ali's next fight was against American Jimmy Young. The day of the fight, Ali weighed in at 230 pounds the heaviest he'd ever been in the ring. It was obvious that Ali hadn't trained seriously for the match, and the boring bout lasted all fifteen rounds, the crowd's boos getting stronger as the fight went on. Ali was declared the winner by unanimous decision, but even trainer Angelo Dundee called the fight the "worst of his career."

Ali knew he had let down his fans, and he arrived in better shape for his next fight only three weeks later against the English boxer Richard Dunn. Ali knocked down Dunn five times before winning the bout in the fifth round. It was the last time that Ali would ever knock an opponent down during a fight.

By this point in his career, Ali's life outside the ring was receiving more attention than his work inside it. In August of 1976, Ali's girlfriend Veronica Porche gave birth to the boxer's seventh child, a daughter named Hana. This was the final straw for his wife Belinda, who asked for a divorce in September.

That same month, Ali took part in a bizarre exhibition match. At the time, Ali seemed more interested in creating excitement than in simply boxing, so he traveled to Tokyo to fight a Japanese wrestler named Antonio Inoki in an event that promoters promised would be watched by millions around the globe. What was billed as the War of the Worlds ended up being a major embarrassment for Ali. Inoki, scared of being

A mixed-sport exhibition in Tokyo against Japanese wrestler Antonio Inoki turned out to be a draw. Worse than that, it was an embarrassment for Ali and a financial disaster for the promoters.

knocked out, spent almost the entire match on his back, kicking Ali's shins every time the champion tried to approach. Ali hoped the stunt would be a worldwide hit, but instead it was a financial disaster.

Soon after, Ali fought Ken Norton for a third time. Having already fought Norton twice, Ali trained like his old self, knowing he was in for a battle. A battle he got, and Norton began the match by pummeling the slower and older Ali. Ali gamely fought back, and Norton, who thought he had the fight won, coasted through the final rounds. Much to both Norton's and the crowd's surprise, the judges awarded Ali a split-decision win.

Ali was still champion, but few believed he was still the best Heavyweight fighter.

The Beginning of the End

In 1977, Ali continued to focus his attention on projects outside of the ring. In June, he married Veronica Porche in Los Angeles. Hoping to make enough money to retire and support both his new wife's love of luxury and his own group of trainers and followers, Ali appeared in advertisements, including some for a cockroach-killing powder, and a movie about his life called *The Greatest*. He also appeared with Superman in the comic book *Superman vs. Muhammad Ali: The Fight to Save Earth from Star-Warriors*. In the story, Ali was forced to box Superman. He beat the superhero in the comic, but in real life, Ali's heroic powers were crumbling quickly.

Ali fought only two times that year. His first fight was against a weak Spanish boxer named Alfredo Evangelista who had no right fighting for the championship. Still, Ali failed to knock out the inexperienced fighter, and the bout went all fifteen rounds

Ali's fame spread beyond the boxing ring in the 1970s. In this photo from 1978, he samples a peanut-butter-and-crisped-rice candy bar named for him.

before Ali was awarded the decision. Howard Cosell, a famed television sport announcer and friend of Ali, was disgusted. "It was one of the worst fights ever fought. . . . The fact that the bout went fifteen rounds told you that Ali was shot."

Then in September, Ali battled Ernie Shavers in a fifteen-round bout at New York's Madison Square Garden. In the second round, the hard-punching Shavers landed a powerful right-handed blow that Ali later described as the second hardest punch he'd ever been hit with. Ali fought back. Round after round, the two men traded blows. Barely able to stand at the end of the final round, Ali was awarded the win by judges' decision. Ali had won, but at what cost?

When he was younger, Ali used his quickness to escape from being hit. With his hands held low, daring opponents to hit him, Ali would duck and dodge punches with the grace and precision of a dancer. But at the age of thirty-five, he now let those same punches land, hoping his opponents would eventually become too tired to keep throwing more. Early in Ali's career, experts believed he had what's called a **glass jaw**—that he would fall after the first big punch. He was now proving that he could take a punch, but each punch chipped away at his health.

Was winning another fight worth the damage it caused? One of the most important men in Ali's camp, Dr. Ferdie Pacheco, believed the answer was no. After the Shavers fight, Pacheco refused to work with Ali any longer. Pacheco had medical evidence that Ali's kidneys were being damaged, and he let the champ know about it. "I didn't want to be a part of what was going on anymore. By then, they were talking about 'only easy fights,' but there was no such thing as an easy fight anymore."

Two against Spinks

Ali's next fight, against Leon Spinks, proved Pacheco right. Spinks had recently won a gold medal for the United States at the 1976 Olympics in Montreal, Canada. Ali wanted to fight Spinks because he had beaten a string of gold-medal winners— Floyd Patterson, Joe Frazier, and George Foreman—and wanted to add one more to his list. That the young Spinks had only fought a handful of professional fights also helped persuade Ali to fight, as did the $3.5 million payday.

The fight on February 15, 1978, was supposed to be an easy match as Spinks was young and had little professional experience. Ali relied on his rope-a-dope strategy once the fight began, letting Spinks fire off punches and waiting until he tired out. However, the younger boxer never did tire out. Instead, Ali was the more exhausted boxer at the final bell. Spinks won the fight by the judges' decision. For only the third time in his career, Ali had lost a fight. This time, he also lost his championship to Spinks.

Unheralded Leon Spinks upset Ali in their fight in 1978 when the younger boxer was not tired by Ali's rope-a-dope tactics. Here, Spinks enjoys his victory as he is named the new Heavyweight champion of the world.

Ali quickly demanded a rematch. "It was embarrassing that someone with so little fighting skills could beat me. . . . I wanted to get my title back. What they paid me didn't matter. I just couldn't leave boxing that way, losing an embarrassing fight like that." To Ali's credit, he trained as hard as he had in years for his rematch with Spinks on September 15, 1978. Every morning, Ali jogged up to five miles, and he sparred nonstop. No longer a young man, Ali was in pain nearly every waking moment. Again, the fight lasted all fifteen rounds, but this time Ali was declared the winner. He had won the championship for the third time.

Soon after the fight, Ali told a writer that he'd "be the biggest fool in the world to go out a loser after being the first three-time champ." On June 26, 1979, nine months after winning the title back, Ali officially announced his retirement from boxing. He moved into a mansion in Los Angeles with his wife Veronica to begin living the good life.

A Graceless Exit

Unfortunately, the good life in Los Angeles turned out to be more expensive than Ali imagined. Out of all the millions of dollars he had made in his career, precious little was left. Some of the money Ali spent on his family that, with the birth of daughter Laila in December of 1977, included eight children and two ex-wives. Much of it he gave way to charities and needy people. In addition, a good deal was taken by people claiming to be Ali's friends, whether it was by terrible business deals or by outright theft. However it happened, Ali was dangerously close to going broke.

To earn a living, Ali acted in a television movie, went on a speaking tour of Europe, and even flew around the world on

Laila Ali

It's not unusual for children to follow in their parents' footsteps. However, because a professional women's boxing league didn't even exist when Ali's youngest daughter, Laila, was born in 1977, it's unlikely that Ali ever thought she would become a boxer too. In 1999, Laila did just that by stepping into the ring as a professional boxer for the first time. Within three years, she had become the world champion Super Middleweight. Along with a successful boxing career, Laila has also appeared on several television shows, including *Dancing with the Stars*, making her the most famous of Ali's nine children.

This photograph shows Laila Ali in 2007. Muhammad's daughter grew up to be a championship boxer, and then a television star.

Ali is pictured here in 1980 with his daughter Laila. She was born to Ali and Veronica Porche in December 1977.

diplomatic missions. However, none of these activities could add up to the type of money he could make by boxing. More than a year after losing to Spinks, Ali returned to the ring on October 2, 1980, to fight the Heavyweight champion at that time, Larry Holmes, for $8 million. (After Ali's "retirement," Holmes had been named the champ by boxing authorities.) The two boxers had known each other for years, with Holmes having previously worked as one of Ali's sparring partners.

While some in Ali's camp cheered him on, many warned him not to step into the ring. Ali's mother was scared for his health, and even Holmes—who considered Ali a mentor and hero— didn't want to fight the former champion. Yet, the money was just too much for Holmes to pass up.

As the day of the fight approached, more concerned voices began speaking out. Ali was beginning to slur his words, and his movements were slowing. The former champion, though, passed a physical before the fight, and the Nevada State Athletic Commission approved the bout.

Ali had trained hard and weighed in at a slim 217 pounds for the fight. His looks, however, were deceiving. Ali was simply too old and too slow to stand a chance. As Ali's biographer wrote, "it wasn't a fight; it was an execution." Round after round, Holmes rained punches down on Ali, battering the former champion. Years later, Ali himself would admit that he knew he was in trouble from the very first round. He just didn't have the speed to keep up with the younger, stronger boxer. Unable to watch any longer, Angelo Dundee stopped the fight after the tenth round.

Ali was beginning to slur his words, and his movements were slowing.

After losing to Holmes, Ali returned to Los Angeles. There was no shame in losing to a younger, skilled boxer such as Holmes. Still, Ali couldn't get over his last bout ending with him still sitting on the stool in his corner, dazed and beaten. That was no way for a champion to finish his career, and his thoughts soon turned to another fight. However, with Ali's health becoming worse, there wasn't a state in America that dared approve another fight.

Ali's camp moved around the problem by organizing a fight against Trevor Berbick in the Bahamas on December 11, 1981. The thirty-nine-year-old Ali, who walked instead of ran during much of his prefight training, weighed in for the fight at 236 pounds and looked terrible. His boxing was even worse, and

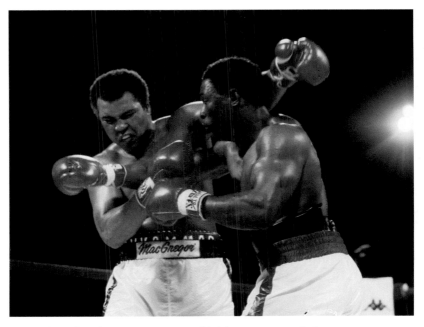

In this fight in the Bahamas in 1981, 39-year-old Ali lost to Trevor Berbick. It was a poorly contested battle, after which Ali retired for good.

the much younger Berbick won the ugly ten-round fight by decision.

The day after the fight, Ali finally admitted what the rest of the world already knew. "Father Time has caught up with me. I'm finished. I've got to face the facts. For the first time, I feel like I'm forty years old. I know it's the end; I'm not crazy."

This time, Ali was true to his word. He would never fight again.

CHAPTER 12

A Champion in Retirement

Muhammad isn't my property. Muhammad belongs to the world.

—Lonnie Williams

The years following Muhammad Ali's retirement from boxing were some of the darkest, most difficult days of his life. Living in Los Angeles with his wife, Veronica, and several of his children, Ali planned on having a peaceful retirement from fighting. Things didn't work out that way, however, and visitors to his Los Angeles mansion often came away saddened, feeling that Ali was both lonely and becoming more unwell. Like a captain without his ship, Ali was lost without his boxing career to guide him.

Like a captain without his ship, Ali was lost without his boxing career to guide him.

First, there were the money problems. Ali was never very careful with his winnings. Generous to a fault, he would lend money to almost anyone who asked and rarely requested repayment. Once, after watching a news story about a retirement home in danger of being closed, Ali anonymously donated enough money to keep it open. He also invested in business deals that, more often than not, failed spectacularly. Without the huge paychecks from his boxing matches coming to him, Ali was beginning to run out of money.

Even more troubling was Ali's health. His hands were trembling frequently and he often found it difficult to speak clearly. Even walking was becoming a problem. In September 1984, Ali checked into a New York City hospital for testing. Soon after, he was officially diagnosed as suffering from Parkinson's syndrome, a medical disorder closely linked to Parkinson's disease. Most medical experts who examined Ali believed that his Parkinson's syndrome was caused by damage to his brain cells from years and years of taking blows to the head in the boxing ring. It was crushing news for Ali, as there is no known cure for Parkinson's. However, doctors informed Ali that, with a steady dose of medication, he could still live a productive life.

Ali jokingly boxes actor Michael J. Fox in hearings before a U.S. Senate subcommittee in 2002. The men were there to talk about Parkinson's. (Ali has been diagnosed with Parkinson's syndrome, and Fox with Parkinson's disease.)

Parkinson's Syndrome

Because of being punched in the head repeatedly over many years, older boxers often begin having problems with their memory, movements, and even speaking. This disorder is sometimes known as being punch drunk. Toward the end of Ali's boxing career, many people believed he was suffering from being punch drunk. Medical testing, however, revealed that Ali's declining health was due to an even more serious illness called Parkinson's syndrome. Those suffering from Parkinson's syndrome deal with the same effects as from Parkinson's disease, including impaired movement, slurred speech, tremors, and a difficulty in remembering words. Unlike Parkinson's disease, which is caused by chemical problems in the brain, Parkinson's syndrome is believed to be caused by actions like the blows to the head Ali received throughout his boxing career.

In addition to Ali's health and money worries, his marriage to Veronica was falling apart. In July of 1986, the couple officially divorced. It seemed that only darker days were ahead for Ali.

A New Life

Newly divorced and facing a serious health challenge, Ali once again proved that while he might be down, he certainly was not out. And this time, he had a new partner to provide him with extra strength. Her name was Lonnie Williams, and she had known Ali since she was five years old, when her parents moved into a home across the street from Ali's parents' house in Louisville. They had long been friends, and on November 19, 1986, the two were married in a small, private ceremony in Louisville.

Just as Angelo Dundee had trained Ali to be the best boxer possible, it was Williams who helped Ali to be the best person possible in retirement. College-educated and experienced in the business world, Williams worked on ending Ali's poor business deals, bringing his money problems to a close. Williams also closely monitored Ali's health and medicine—which he sometimes avoided taking—helping keep his Parkinson's syndrome symptoms in check. And though raised as a Roman Catholic, Williams converted to Ali's religion of Islam, making their relationship spiritually strong as well. In 1991, Ali and

Ali and Lonnie Williams, shown here in 1990, were friends since their youth. They were married in 1986.

Williams adopted a newborn baby boy—the youngest of Ali's nine children in total—and named him Assad Amin Ali.

With Williams by his side, Ali slowly emerged from the haze of his early retirement. Williams knew that being around people was important to the former world champion, and she made sure Ali kept a busy schedule of appearances around the world. "Muhammad loves people and loves having people around him," Williams once explained. "Muhammad isn't my property. Muhammad belongs to the world."

Refusing to let Parkinson's control him, to this day Ali continues to seek out the spotlight, using his fame and popularity to spread peace and happiness. In 1998, Ali's tireless work was honored by the United Nations with the Messenger of Peace award, given to those who work on ending violence

Even as he battles health problems, Muhammad Ali remains a goodwill ambassador around the world. In this picture, he greets fans in the Ivory Coast of Africa.

and bringing the world closer together. "I like traveling because it gives me a chance to meet people and see different things," says Ali. "There are billions of people in the world, and every one of them is special." Whether attending a boxing awards dinner in his honor or making a surprise appearance at a charity event halfway across the globe, the

"There are billions of people in the world, and every one of them is special."

nearly seventy-year-old Ali spends more than two hundred days a year traveling and visiting with fans. Just like when he went home to Louisville with his Olympic gold medal in 1960, Ali still draws large crowds wherever he goes.

Although Parkinson's makes it difficult for Ali to talk or change his facial expressions, mentally he's as strong as ever. "I don't want anyone to feel sorry for me, because I had a good life before and I'm having a good life now," Ali once explained after being asked about his illness. "I accept it at God's will. And I know God never gives anyone a burden that's too heavy for them to carry."

At home, Ali and Williams have settled into a content routine. Religion is as important for Ali as it ever was, and he prays at least five times a day. He also signs hundreds of Islamic pamphlets daily so he can hand them out to those he meets.

Two events in particular stand out as highlights in Ali's postboxing career. On July 19, 1996, Ali lit the Olympic flame at the opening of the Summer Games in Atlanta, Georgia. Billions of viewers around the world watched as Ali, shaking but with his head held high, was honored by being the last to carry the Olympic Torch and light the flame. And on November 19, 2005, Ali attended the opening ceremony of the Muhammad Ali Center in Louisville, a dream come true for many of Ali's greatest fans.

In a memorable scene, Ali lights the Olympic flame at the Opening Ceremonies of the 1996 Games in Atlanta, Georgia.

Looking back at the incredible life of Muhammad Ali, it's clear that he has been not only a one-of-a-kind athlete but also a one-of-a-kind man. Here is a person who once claimed he was "so mean he'd make medicine sick," yet his life is dedicated to faith and healing. Here is a man who dished out tremendous punishment within the boxing ring but who also spread joy to the world outside of it. Here is a man who grew up as a

The Muhammad Ali Center

Opened in 2005, the Muhammad Ali Center is a fitting tribute to a larger-than-life hero. Built on the banks of the Ohio River in downtown Louisville, the six-story center is more than just a museum dedicated to Ali's life. It's also an educational center, with the goal of inspiring adults and children to be as great as they can be. Of course, visitors are also treated to footage of Ali's greatest fights, a re-creation of his Deer Lake training camp, and loads of memorabilia, ranging from a fancy Rolls-Royce convertible that he drove, to the torch Ali used to light the flame at the 1996 Summer Olympics.

second-class citizen in a segregated society but who learned to love and treat everyone as equals. Ali certainly wasn't perfect in his life in and out of the ring—no man ever could be. However, he was, and always will be, the Greatest.

I'll tell you how I'd like to be remembered: as a black man who won the heavyweight title and who was humorous and who treated everyone right. As a man who never looked down on those who looked up to him and who helped as many of his people as he could. . . . As a man who tried to unite his people through the faith of Islam that he found when he listened to the honorable Elijah Muhammad. And if all that's asking too much, then I guess I'd settle for being remembered as only a great boxing champion who became a preacher and a champion of his people. And I wouldn't even mind if folks forgot how pretty I was.

Glossary

abolitionist—a person who fought against slavery when it was legal in the United States.

amateur—one who does something without getting paid; the opposite of a professional.

ambassador—one who represents his or her country or a special cause.

bail—a payment, usually money, used to keep a person out of jail while on trial.

bout—another boxing term for a match or a fight.

boycott—to refuse to take part in something as a way to protest against it.

civil rights movement—a worldwide political movement aimed at obtaining equal rights for all.

communism—a form of government based on a classless society; during the cold war, the U.S. government considered communism to be an evil force.

cornerman—a person who coaches a boxer and gives instructions between rounds.

draft—an order to join a country's military service.

entourage—a group of supporters. For boxers, this would include trainers, managers, cornermen, friends, and others.

ghetto—a poor, often rundown neighborhood.

glass jaw—the boxing term for someone who is knocked down easily.

hernia—an internal injury of the intestines and abdominal muscles.

hook—a powerful sideways punch that swings around an opponent's defense.

integration—the act of bringing people together, with equal rights and access to all.

jabs—the boxing term for snappy, less powerful punches.

journeyman—a longtime boxer of average to below-average skill.

Mosque—a Muslim place of worship; the equivalent of a Christian church or a Jewish synagogue.

novice—an inexperienced person; a rookie.

prostrate—to lie low or flat on the ground.

round—a three-minute period into which a boxing match is divided.

segregating—keeping people of different groups, usually different races or religions, separate.

sharecroppers—farmers who don't own the land but rent it from someone else and share in the harvest.

smelling salts—a chemical compound used to wake stunned or knocked-out boxers.

sparring partner—a training-camp partner used by boxers to imitate a real fight.

split decision—how the winner of a boxing match is declared when the judges do not all agree who won.

sponsor—a person or group that supports someone else's career or training.

uppercut—a powerful upward punch, often aimed at an opponent's chin.

Viet-cong—an army based in Vietnam that fought against both the United States and the South Vietnamese government during the Vietnam War.

Bibliography

Brunt, Stephen. *Facing Ali: 15 Fighters, 15 Stories*. Guilford, CT: The Lyons Press, 2002.

Hauser, Thomas. *Muhammad Ali: His Life and Times*. New York: Simon & Schuster, 1991.

Kram, Mark. "For Blood and For Money." *Sports Illustrated*, September 29, 1975

———. "Lawdy, Lawdy, He's Great." *Sports Illustrated*, October 13, 1975.

———. "The Battered Face of a Winner." *Sports Illustrated*, March 15, 1971.

Kreeps, Alan. "Muhammad Ali, Guest on Capitol Hill, Meets President." *New York Times*, December 11, 1974.

Myers, Walter Dean. *The Greatest: Muhammad Ali*. New York: Scholastic, 2001.

Nack, William. "Young Cassius Clay." *Sports Illustrated*, January 13, 1992.

Olsen Jack. "A Case of Conscience." *Sports Illustrated*, April 11, 1966.

Plimpton, George. "Breaking a Date for the Dance." *Sports Illustrated*, November 11, 1974

————. *Shadow Box: An Amateur in the Ring*. New York: Putnam, 1977.

————. "Watching the Man in the Mirror," *Sports Illustrated*, November 23, 1970.

Remnick, David. *King of the World: Muhammad Ali and the Rise of the American Hero*. New York: Vintage, 1998.

When We Were Kings, DVD. Directed by Leon Gast. Polygram USA Video, 2002.

Source Notes

The following citations list the sources of quoted material in this book. The first and last few words of each quotation are cited and followed by their source. Complete information on the referenced sources can be found in the Bibliography.

Abbreviations:
BDD—"Breaking a Date for the Dance"
BFW—"The Battered Face of a Winner"
COC—"A Case of Conscience"
FA—*Facing Ali: 15 Fighters, 15 Stories*
FCFM—"For Blood and For Money"
KW—*King of the World: Muhammad Ali and the Rise of the American Hero*
LL—"Lawdy, Lawdy, He's Great"
MAG—"Muhammad Ali, Guest on Capitol Hill, Meets President"
MALT—*Muhammad Ali: His Life and Times*
SB—*Shadow Box: An Amateur in the Ring*
TG—*The Greatest: Muhammad Ali*
WWWK—*When We Were Kings*
YCC—"Young Cassius Clay"

INTRODUCTION: King of the World
  PAGE 1 *"I am the king! . . . King of the world!"*: KW, p. 200
  PAGE 1 *"I am the king! . . . King of the world!"*: KW, p. 200

CHAPTER 1: The Louisville Lip
  PAGE 2 *"His mind . . . proved me wrong."*: MALT, p. 16
  PAGE 4 *"He was . . . in my mouth."*: KW, p. 84
  PAGES 4–5 *"She taught us . . . with kindness."*: MALT, p. 14
  PAGES 5–6 *"I'd come . . . all the talking."*: KW, p. 84
  PAGE 8 *"If we were . . . we didn't belong."*: MALT, p. 17

CHAPTER 2: Good as Gold

CHAPTER 3: A Brash Beginning

CHAPTER 4: A King Is Crowned

PAGES 37–38 *"For all the joking . . . in his way,":* KW, p. 187

PAGE 38 *"float like a butterfly, sting like a bee.":* SB, p. 302

PAGE 38 *"Come on, you bum,":* KW, p. 193

PAGE 38 *"Come on, you bum,":* KW, p. 193

PAGE 39 *"I am the king! . . . King of the world!":* KW, p. 200

CHAPTER 5: The Name's Ali, Muhammad Ali

PAGE 40 *"A rooster crows . . . I'm crowing.":* MALT, p. 83

PAGE 40 *"blue-eyed devils,":* KW, p. 127

PAGE 42 *"He invited . . . my life changed,":* MALT, p. 89

PAGES 42–43 *"You can't . . . I'm crowing.":* MALT, p. 83

PAGE 44 *"Changing my name . . . beautiful name.":* MALT, p. 102

PAGE 44 *"Changing my name . . . in my life.":* MALT, p. 102

PAGES 47/49 *"the phantom punch":* MALT, p. 127

PAGE 48 *"Ali thought . . . said made sense,":* KW, p. 165

PAGE 48 *"little brother,":* MALT, p. 100

PAGE 48 *"It was a . . . mind that counts.":* MALT, pp. 111–112

PAGE 49 *"Get up and fight, sucker.":* MALT, p. 127

CHAPTER 6: Banished from Boxing

PAGE 50 *"Man, I ain't . . . them Viet-cong.":* KW, p. 287

PAGE 50 *"I said I . . . the smartest,":* COC

PAGE 51 *"I have nothing . . . and the nation.":* MALT, p. 139

PAGE 52 *"Man, I ain't . . . them Viet-cong.":* KW, p. 287

PAGE 52 *"Man, I ain't . . . them Viet-cong.":* KW, p. 287

PAGE 52 *"sorry spectacle.":* MALT, p. 145

PAGE 52 *"squealed like a cornered rat":* MALT, p. 145

PAGES 52–53 *"never go to . . . be ashamed.":* MALT p. 147

PAGE 55 *"How can I . . . times a day for peace?":* MALT, p. 155

PAGE 56 *"What's my name!":* TG, p. 58

PAGE 57 *"I never thought . . . as brave as I did.":* MALT, p. 171

PAGES 58–59 *"He was, and is, . . . born with it on.":* MALT, p. 178

PAGES 59–60 *"blue-eyed devils":* KW, p. 127

PAGE 60 *"Some say I . . . willing to back up.":* WWWK

CHAPTER 7: The Fight of the Century

PAGE 61 *"This might shock . . . Joe Frazier.":* MALT, p. 222

PAGE 62 *"You best be . . . whole wide world.":* BDD

PAGE 63 *"I don't think . . . was Joe Frazier.":* MALT, p. 326

PAGE 64 *"Joe's gonna . . . destroy Joe Frazier.":* MALT, p. 222

PAGES 64–65 *"There's not a . . . ever get licked.":* MALT, p. 223

PAGE 65 *"Anything that . . . still hurts.":* FA, p. 120

PAGE 67 *"draped over each . . . wallowed onto a beach.":* BFW

PAGE 67 *"The way they were . . . I've ever seen."*: BFW
PAGE 67 *"Let's get out. . . . Let's go home."*: SB, p. 188
PAGE 67 *"You're a real tough man."*: SB, p. 188
PAGE 67 *"You are too. You're the champ."*: SB, p. 188

CHAPTER 8: Warrior Spirit
PAGE 68 *"I lost it. . . . not ashamed."*: SB, p. 205
PAGES 68–69 *"Oh, they all . . . I'm not ashamed."*: SB, p. 205
PAGE 70 *"people's champion."*: MALT, p. 253
PAGE 74 *"I took a . . . punish him bad."*: MALT, p. 253
PAGE 75 *"There's something . . screws someplace."*: MALT, p. 255
PAGE 76 *"I'm not gonna . . . chances he wants."*: MALT, p. 258

CHAPTER 9: The Rumble in the Jungle
PAGE 77 *"I'm so mean I make medicine sick."*: MALT, pp. 269–270
PAGE 81 *"Ali, bomma-ya."*: TG, p. 118
PAGE 81 *"I never get . . . fellow, it's over."*: MALT, p. 267
PAGE 81 *"I never get . . . fellow, it's over."*: MALT, p. 267
PAGE 81 *"he moves like . . . Muhammad Ali."*: MALT, p. 266
PAGE 81 *"a bad morning shave."*: MALT, p. 266
PAGE 82 *"Float like a . . . make medicine sick."*: SB, p. 302
PAGE 82 *"Ali, bomma-ya."*: TG, p. 118
PAGE 83 *"This ain't nothing . . . in the gym."*: BDD
PAGE 83 *"I won't kid . . . ropes, I felt sick."*: MALT, p. 276
PAGE 84 *"Is that the . . . a sissy punch."*: SB, p. 326
PAGE 84 *"Ali, . . . bomma-ya"*: TG, p. 118
PAGE 85 *"I realized I'd . . . him a lot."*: MALT, p. 278

CHAPTER 10: The World's Champion
PAGE 86 *[Ali almost] . . . meant to be loved."*: MALT, p. 286
PAGE 87 *"You made a . . after your job."*: MAG
PAGES 87–88 *"Most celebrities . . . to be loved."*: MALT, p. 286
PAGE 90 *"Wallace is showing . . . hate people."*: MALT, p. 295
PAGE 93 *"It will be . . . in Manila."*: MALT, p. 314
PAGE 93 *"It's real . . . his heart out."*: FCFM
PAGE 94 *"Old Joe Frazier, . . were washed up,"*: LL
PAGE 94 *"Somebody told you all wrong, pretty boy,"*: LL
PAGE 95 *"Sit down, son . . . did here today."*: LL
PAGE 95 *"Frazier quit . . . I could fight anymore."*: MALT, p. 324
PAGE 95 *"He's the greatest . . . Next to me."*: FA, p. 123

CHAPTER 11: Throwing in the Towel
PAGE 96 *"For the first time . . . I'm not crazy."*: MALT, p. 430
PAGE 97 *"worst of his career."*: MALT, p. 333

Image Credits

About the Author

Stephen Timblin, an award-winning author and editor, has long admired Muhammad Ali's remarkable boxing skills and inspiring inner strength. Timblin has written several sports books covering everything from motocross and NASCAR to the history of swimming. An experienced travel writer, he is co-author of the *Rough Guide to Skiing and Snowboarding* and sole author of the *Rough Guide to Yellowstone and Grand Teton*. He lives with his wife, twin daughters, dog, and two cats in Detroit, Michigan.

Index